L O V E D A L E

LOVEDALE

SOUTH AFRICA

ILLUSTRATED BY

FIFTY VIEWS FROM PHOTOGRAPHS

WITH INTRODUCTION BY

JAMES STEWART, D.D., M.D., HON. F.R.G.S.

EDINBURGH
ANDREW ELLIOT: 17 PRINCES STREET
GLASGOW: DAVID BRYCE AND SON

1894

Edinburgh : T. and A. CONSTABLE, Printers to Her Majesty

TO THE RIGHT HONOURABLE

SIR GEORGE GREY, K.C.B.

ETC. ETC. ETC.

FORMERLY GOVERNOR OF

HER MAJESTY'S POSSESSIONS IN THE COLONY OF

THE CAPE OF GOOD HOPE

UNDER WHOSE ADMINISTRATION AND BY WHOSE AID THE FIRST STEPS

WERE TAKEN TO TEACH THE ARTS OF CIVILISED LIFE

TO THE NATIVE RACES OF SOUTH AFRICA

THIS BRIEF RECORD OF SUCH WORK IS RESPECTFULLY

DEDICATED

PREFACE

LLUSTRATION seems to be a necessity of the present day. It saves time in reading, and conveys a certain clearness of impression. These views accordingly have been prepared for the information of the friends and supporters of the Lovedale Mission, as well as of others who may be interested in the progress of Christian missions generally. It would be difficult, if not hopeless, amidst the torrent of books annually issuing from the British press, to expect to interest any circle of readers by a volume of letterpress description merely, on any single mission. Hence the method of illustration adopted.

The following pages are a transcript and issue in a cheap form, of a volume of letterpress and photographs prepared for a limited circulation.

There has been some request for such information. What is here given may supply that want.

It was to Sir George Grey, K.C.B., while Governor of the Cape Colony, that the industrial section of that work owed its origin ; and on his recommendation the first pecuniary aid of £3000 was given to commence the necessary operations. The main features of Sir George Grey's wise and humane native policy were these :—To combat superstition by promoting Christianity ; to shake native faith in witchcraft, and those who practised it by skilled medical aid ; to overcome ignorance by native schools ; and to counteract indolence by industrial training in various trades, and by employment on works of public utility.

And to Sir Langham Dale, recently Superintendent-General of Education in the Colony, Lovedale and many similar places owe a great deal for his generous encouragement and support.

This Introduction is partly a descriptive and condensed account of Lovedale, and partly a plea for the method followed there. That may be called the combined method, in which religious, educational, and industrial teaching are conjoined with the preaching of the Gospel, or the purely evangelistic method. The latter must always take the chief and most honoured place.

In support of this form of missionary operations the views of Mackay of Uganda and others have been freely quoted. Whatever opinion may be entertained as to the fitness of this combined method as applied to other fields, it seems necessary to the widest kind of success in missionary work in the African Continent.

These introductory pages also contain an appeal for a new arm of the missionary service—an auxiliary force—in the shape of a volunteer, unpaid, or honorary contingent. There are signs that this appeal may not be made in vain and that such a force, when duly organised, will yet become an important agency in the great work of the world's evangelisation.

Sometimes I have expressed the opinion of my colleagues as well as my own, and at others only my individual view. This may explain some varying forms of expression.

JAMES STEWART.

LOVEDALE, SOUTH AFRICA, 1894.

CONTENTS

L O V E D A L E

CHAPTER I

INTRODUCTION

THESE reproductions from photographs are intended to give the friends and supporters of the Mission, as well as others, some representation of Lovedale and its surroundings. The letterpress which accompanies each view, as well as this Introduction, will afford some information about the place, its gradual progress, and the different kinds of work carried on. Numerous as the views are, they are only a portion of what might have been given. There are in all twenty-five separate buildings. The site which the missionaries received was at first a bare hill-side and a flat valley covered with mimosa trees. The change has been effected by the aid of the friends of missions, who have supported the labours of the missionaries.

REALITIES OF MISSIONARY WORK

The realities of Missionary work are generally different from what they are supposed by many at home to be. The work itself requires much patience, and the progress is not usually very rapid. Some are not satisfied with missionary reports and addresses unless they contain more or less of the picturesque and marvellous, either in personal incident or achievement. There are, indeed, marvels in the transformation of character when the Gospel takes effect, as every missionary knows, but they do not lend themselves very readily to highly-wrought description. These great changes belong to the kingdom that comes not with observation; and the record often is as brief as it is important.   What, however, the most intelligent supporters of missions chiefly desire is—reliable figures, moderate and accurate statements, and definitely achieved results.

Such results should always be given,—though they may be less than the missionary and the home public desire and expect,—rather than indefinite predictions and great expectations lying always in the future.   The great future of the missionary enterprise may be left to take care of itself.   It is safe in the hands of its Founder.   Its progress means the gradual spread of Christianity.   Its final success means, that the future religion of mankind will be the religion of Jesus Christ, and the future civilisation of the world a Christian civilisation, whatever its form may be.   Many at the presᵉ day do not believe this, and think missions and Christianity itseᵢᵢ forces.   Unless, however, not only the Bible but human history are both misread, the purpose of God about this world seems to be, that the religion founded by Jesus Christ shall yet become the universal faith of mankind.

ALOES COMING INTO FLOWER.   THE GIGANTIC SPIKE IS THE GROWTH MOSTLY OF ONE SEASON.

CHAPTER II

LOVEDALE—HISTORY, AIMS, AND METHOD

WHY SO NAMED

T was so called after a man who, when missions were less popular than they are now, did much to stir up interest in them—the Rev. Dr. Love of Glasgow. He was one of the early secretaries of the famous London Missionary Society, and also one of the founders of the old Glasgow Missionary Society. The latter no longer exists, though it was one of the first to send missionaries to Africa, both West and South. This is the origin of the name, and it was not given from any sentimental reason, or because the place was some Happy Valley, where love was more common than elsewhere; though it is the want of that best of all possessions which often makes the earth so bare, our lives so poor, and our Christianity so feeble.

WHERE IT IS

Lovedale lies about 700 miles north-east of Cape Town, and about 80 miles due west of the Indian Ocean, on the edge of what was once independent Kaffraria, the home of the Kaffir race before they became British subjects. But so many and so great have been the changes since then, that British South and Central Africa now extends in one unbroken line to the north of Lake Nyassa, that is, nearly twenty degrees nearer the equator than the old colonial boundary line. Within this large area lie the Orange Free State and the Transvaal Republic; while to the east and west on the coast line, lie some portions of Portuguese and German territory.

Real Africa is indeed a very different country from the conventional Africa of not very many years ago. The mental picture usually then formed was that of a vast sandy arid plain, with a palm tree, a black man, and the ubiquitous lion or snake. The country round Lovedale does not answer to this conception. Towards the south and west it consists of undulating hills, and broad valleys with numerous streams and small rivers; while immediately to the north rises the striking range of mountains known as the Amatolas, the Katberg, and Winterberg. The highest of these reaches an elevation of 7000 feet. Snow is occasionally seen on their tops during winter, just as it is seen, on account of an altitude, all the year, on the summits of Kilimanjaro and Kenia, though these lie almost under the equator. No doubt travellers who pass through South Africa from Cape Town to Kimberley and Johannesburg, and who traverse the great Karoo on the west with its almost waterless expanse, think that conventional Africa of bygone days is still the reality. But the eastern side of Southern Africa presents a great and favourable contrast to that of the west.

There were no railways in South Africa in the early days of the Mission, though there are now over 2000 miles already constructed and more in process of formation. The nearest point where any line passes, is about forty miles distant from the Mission station.

KINDS OF WORK CARRIED ON

Missionary work at Lovedale is carried on mainly on three lines—religious, educational, and industrial. Medical work, to some slight extent, was at one time attempted, but given up for want of funds.

As a missionary place, it seeks spiritual results as its highest and most permanent result, and as its primary aim. If the will and conscience are right, the man will be right. Its chief aim, therefore, is not to civilise, but to Christianise. Merely to civilise can never be the primary aim of the missionary. Civilisation without Christianity among a savage people is a mere matter of clothes and whitewash. But among barbarous races a sound missionary method will in every way endeavour to promote civilisation by education and industry, resting on the solid foundation of religious instruction. Hence there is a variety of teaching.

EDUCATIONAL WORK

The range of education is considerable. It begins with the alphabet in the elementary school, and ends in theological classes for native ministers and missionaries. The object of this section of work is to prepare preachers and evangelists for native congregations ; to supply teachers for mission schools ; and to give a general education to all who seek it and who are willing to pay for it. There can be no doubt or hesitation about the soundness of this method. All other things being equal, the man who can read and write, even if he be a wagon-driver, will be a more useful man than he who cannot, whatever be the colour of his skin. Books and pure barbarism, with its low conditions of life—generally the minimum of existence—are incompatible things.

INDUSTRIAL WORK

Among a people in barbarism, or emerging from it, there is almost entire ignorance of the arts of civilised life and a certain indolence, which is often a serious barrier to the acceptance of the Gospel. There is also the danger of unsatisfactory results, if all that goes on under the name of education is confined to a knowledge of books and attendance at school classes. Knowledge merely puffeth up, but manual labour taught with charity certainly edifieth the individual—in the original sense of that word—as well as the African social state.

The following trades are taught—Carpentering, Wagon-making, Blacksmithing, Printing, Bookbinding, and even Telegraphing ; the latter only to a few. In addition, all who are not indentured to these trades engage in some kind of manual work about the place for a certain number of hours daily, in the gardens or fields, or on the roads, and in keeping the extensive grounds in order. A large farm is also cultivated to supply food, and this affords work in the sowing, hoeing, and reaping seasons, as well as at other times during the year.

NUMBERS

Lovedale, which was founded in 1841 by the Rev. W. Govan, started with eleven natives and nine Europeans, sons of missionaries, for whom at that time the opportunities for education were few. There are now nearly 800 under instruction, in various stages of progress. Of these, 500 are boarders or residents in the place.

INSTITUTION CHURCH

There are two native churches connected with Lovedale, one for the Institution proper, and one for the district. The latter is under the care of a native pastor. Its work involves constant itineration, and maintaining services at distant out-stations. This could not be undertaken by the staff at Lovedale without their neglecting other regular work, though on Sundays a certain number of that staff are always more or less engaged in preaching.

The numbers connected with the Institution itself form an audience of between 500 and 600, and large enough to constitute a small church by themselves. By this, as a part of the regular work, the missionary objects of the place are more fully secured ; and the religious interests and welfare of those who come—many seeking education only—are thus more really cared for. The membership last year was 150 ; of these 21 were received during the year. The class of catechumens numbered 129. The regular membership would be much larger but for the fact of frequent changes, when their course of education is finished. Connected with this Institution Church there is a Missionary Association of native students, the members of which go in small parties on Sundays to the kraals or villages, for a radius of from two to ten miles, and hold services among the heathen natives who do not as yet attend church.

There is also the native church of the district, numbering 700 members, of which the Rev. Pambani Mzimba has been the faithful and successful pastor for seventeen years. This congregation is now almost self-supporting, and will be so entirely in two or three years at most, having been placed on a sliding scale of decreasing annual grant from the home committee.

NATIVE SUPPORT OF THE PLACE BY PAYMENTS

After education had been given free for many years, it was thought, some time ago, that the native people themselves should begin to aid the work and relieve the home church. This would also serve to test the value they set on the education given by missionaries.   In 1871 the system of payment was begun.   The change was not at all popular with the natives, and many European missionaries thought it a dangerous innovation.   But it was necessary, if the place was to grow, as the missionary-contributing home public could not be always expected to find funds for inevitable and beneficial expansion.   For three years we watched for a favourable opportunity.   This occurred at the date mentioned.   It was necessary to carry the natives with us.   It took two entire days' talk to get this new and unpopular change introduced.   The Kaffir's privilege and parliament, is freedom of debate in a public meeting.   He is naturally conservative, believing and asserting that the good old customs of his forefathers are still good enough for him.   This 'new thing' was therefore not well received.   But on the evening of the second day one man—Nyoka (Snake) by name—though his name belied his life—stood up and said, 'I will pay four pounds for my son.'   The others soon followed and a beginning was made, resulting in a great change in the financial condition of Lovedale.   The sum of four pounds a year was what was charged at first; it is now eight pounds.   For this they receive education and food, consisting chiefly of maize and milk.   To this man, Nyoka, now dead, I have many times during these twenty years felt sincerely grateful.

The first year the new system produced only £200.   Last year, and for several previous years, it produced over £2000.   There was a time when the natives did not pay two thousand beads or buttons, though in their earliest days they had to be tempted to attend by presents of brass wire, beads, and buttons, and other such articles of valuable consideration to them at that time.

No better proof can be given of the fitness of the method of education, and their appreciation of it, than the fact that since the change was made, the natives themselves have paid in fees the large sum of over £25,000.

ALL DENOMINATIONS AND MANY TRIBES

Lovedale is almost entirely supported by the Free Church of Scotland, yet it is also entirely unsectarian.   No distinction is made as to privileges or admission—all denominations, tribes, and colours being equally welcome. Natives therefore come from nearly all the missions in the country—from the stations of the Episcopalian, London Missionary Society, Wesleyan, United Presbyterian, French Mission in Basutoland, Moravian, Berlin Missionary Society, and others, as well as from the Free Church Mission. In religious teaching we give prominence to the main truths of the Gospel of Jesus Christ, rather than to unimportant denominational differences between churches which are labouring for the same end. The same rule holds with regard to tribes. The proud Kaffir and the fighting Zulu, and the quieter Barolong, all receive the same treatment so long as there is no fighting. And though the majority are growing lads, and young men and young women, it ought to be stated that in the matter of discipline we have no more trouble than we should have with the same numbers of other and more advanced races.

Representatives of as many as fifteen different tribes were in the place last year. There have been a few from Lake Nyassa and the Shiré; and there is a small body of Gallas, over sixty in number, who were rescued slaves, and come from north of the equator.

MINOR AGENCIES

Besides preaching, teaching, and industrial work, there are various minor agencies connected with the place. There are also two Literary Societies, a Scripture Union, and other associations. There is a good library of over 8000 volumes, issuing 2000 volumes yearly. The Lovedale Post and Telegraph Office has an average of letters, papers, parcels, and messages, forwarded and received of over 51,000 annually. This is exclusive of the monthly issues of the *Christian Express* and *Lovedale News*, two small papers published in the place. And as all Africans are musical, and as relaxation is as necessary as work, there is a good instrumental band.

INCOME AND EXPENDITURE

The average income and expenditure is generally over £10,000 a year. When building is going on, as it almost always is, the expenditure is considerably more. That income is drawn in nearly equal proportions from three sources. These are—Native and European payments as fees for board and education, as there are generally a few Europeans, sons of missionaries, and others resident in the place. There is also the grant allowed by the Education Department of the Cape Government. And there is the annual sum allowed by the Foreign Missions Committee of the Free Church of Scotland. To these amounts must be added any voluntary contributions which may be sent for buildings, general expenditure, or any special object. Such assistance, in a constantly growing place, is always needed. The finance of Lovedale is one of its great difficulties. As it is, seventy per cent. of its average expenditure is raised in South Africa itself; the remainder comes from home.

THE LOVEDALE METHOD

Lovedale is frequently spoken of as a large Educational and Industrial Institution. There is a good deal of such agency, but if that were all, it would be very incomplete as a missionary place; as such, it would indeed be a very poor place. Spiritual results, as has already been stated, are those which are mainly sought after. These form the enduring success and real glory of missionary work, and without them it hardly deserves the name of such work. The reasons for making these results the chief object aimed at have already been given.

But when a certain stage has been reached, the difficulty is to get what may be called, in one word, the ethical side of religious teaching and training sufficiently developed. When persecution has ceased, as it does after a time, or where British law and authority prevail, religious profession becomes comparatively easy. But to secure the further proofs of the reality of such teaching in honest industry, in the expression of uprightness, truth and reality in work as well as in word, that is much more difficult. Practical work must therefore be combined with the religious teaching given. A good Christian should be a good workman up to the point of his natural ability, and as far as his moral sense has been developed and informed. The religion of the African, however, tends to be more or less emotional. It is so, both in Africa and America, though with the more educated in both countries it is becoming less. Emotional results are apt at times to deceive both the man himself and others, and they are therefore less satisfactory evidence of the genuineness and solidity of his religious experience than the practical.

School teaching is given to improve the mind and general intelligence, and industrial work, while it has its value as a civilising end in itself, is also followed with a view to these further practical results. Idleness is no part of Christianity, and is not a satisfactory result of education generally. Hence

B

the combination of the different methods or processes of training; always keeping the chief one, namely, the moral and spiritual change, first in point of importance.

To the question often put—

'Do you civilise or Christianise first? With a people in the entirely uncivilised state, we should think the civilising process ought to come first.'

Our answer is always this—'If possible we avoid doing things twice. When a man is Christianised—that is, when the great change has really taken place in him—he is generally civilised as well; or he will become more so day by day. He will appear clothed, and in his right mind, and the change will continue.'

A CORNER IN THE GARDEN

CHAPTER III

'LOVEDALE: PAST AND PRESENT'

AN Annual Report has been published for the last twenty two years. It records the progress from year to year. Missionary reports are, however, accepted by many with extreme hesitation, and this view may be held by some about the Lovedale Annual Report.

A totally different form of statement exists in a volume entitled *Lovedale: Past and Present.* Its title-page states that it is a 'Record written in Black and White, but more in White than Black.' It is an attempt to give an accurate statement of facts, without the expression of any opinion, about the school, college, and workshop life, and subsequent occupations of those above a certain age who have passed through the place. In that volume of over 650 pages, a product of the Lovedale printing press, over two thousand four hundred brief biographies are given, over a thousand names of juniors being omitted. To record facts and allow others to form their own judgment is the object of that volume. We extenuate nought, not even if the record is not a good one; nor, as might be expected, do we set down aught in malice. The bare facts of that volume, looked at with the eye of human sympathy, form a pathetic record of a struggle, and even of much pecuniary sacrifice, to escape out of the region of entire ignorance, to the edge, at least, of that where knowledge begins. The £25,000 already referred to, must not be forgotten as an indication of sincerity and willingness to pay for their own advancement.

RESULTS AS SHOWN BY SUBSEQUENT OCCUPATIONS

An analysis of the numbers given in that volume shows the different occupations followed after leaving Lovedale. These employments vary from that of wagon-drivers and labourers at railway construction and at the Kimberley mines, to that of ministers to native congregations, and even as editors of native newspapers. Three have been so employed, and the single native newspaper at present published in South Africa, the *Imvo Zabantsundu*, or *Native Opinion*, is entirely managed and ably edited by a native African, and former student of Lovedale.

The volume referred to was published eight years ago. If we add a few figures for the interval, the numbers for the chief occupations stand nearly thus:—Of native ministers and evangelists, including the sons of a few missionaries who have themselves become missionaries, the number is over 50 ; teachers, male and female, over 500 ; tradesmen of various kinds, interpreters and magistrates' clerks, storemen, and those engaged in agricultural work, or on their own land, or in transport work, between 500 and 600. A considerable number fall under the head of miscellaneous and special occupations, while many had to be placed under the head of 'no information.' This will be so far remedied in the second edition.

Do the Natives Make Use of this Education ?

The only answer that can be given to this question, is the figures which form the summaries published in that analysis. What we here vouch for is, that those whose names appear in the pages of that volume are now, or have been, so employed. Of this fact there neither need, nor can, be any doubt, because in most cases we have been able to assign both a local habitation and a name ; and inquiry can be made. There is another kind of proof of the continuance of one class, namely teachers. The mission schools of the country and its frontiers are entirely taught by natives supplied from this and similar institutions. Probably not a dozen Europeans are so employed in all these numerous schools. Further, many of the above 500 have continued long enough at their occupations to receive the 'good-service' allowance from the Education Department of the Cape Government. Many of them also have advanced to better positions, their places being supplied by others. The chief doubt, however, is about the results of industrial education. Therefore the following question, frequently put, also requires an answer.

Do they Work at their Trades after leaving Lovedale?

Yes and No is the answer to this question, according to its full meaning. If it means, Does every one who is taught a trade follow it persistently and work at nothing else?—the answer is No. If it means, Do a reasonable number continue so working?—the answer is Yes. So far as can be ascertained, the numbers and record given correspond to real facts.

Many causes influence their continuance. When trade is depressed, the white man, because he is the better workman, gets the preference. Carpenters, wagon-makers, and blacksmiths are the first to suffer in this way. And it is hardly to be expected that they should not take to other employments, if these are offered. Printers are always in demand; but the number who have as yet been taught printing is so small as to be hardly noticeable when scattered through the country. We also often discover, though sometimes too late even after the year of trial, that many applicants for a trade make very poor workmen. In process of time, therefore, these drop out of the class of native artisans, and are compelled to take to some more common occupation, such as that of day-labourers, at much lower wages. Ordinarily those who continue at their trades easily earn from twenty to thirty shillings a week, and this of itself is sufficient to prevent them sinking to day-labour at one shilling and sixpence a day.

As a matter of fact, if those individuals who have received an industrial training are not following their trades, they will generally be found at some other useful and regular occupation.

Money Wasted on Industrial Grants

The statement is often made that 'industrial grants are simply money wasted on the Kaffir, who never continues at his trade, but prefers to lead an idle life.' If this is intended to apply to all, or even to the majority, it is simply untrue. It is the utterance of languid ignorance, too feeble or too inactive to inform itself; or it is the voice of embittered prejudice. It is equivalent to saying that the individual who has been subjected to the discipline of daily work for four or five years, and of school two or three years previously, in all for seven or eight years, is just as likely to lead for the rest of his days the same kind of life as the raw native leads, in red clay and a blanket. Even when those so taught do not continuously follow their trades, the majority are more industrious and more progressive than those who have received no training. Their slight taste of civilised life, even for these few years, has taught them at least one lesson : it is this, that barbarism has its discomforts as well as civilisation, and that the *ne plus ultra* of existence, or even of comfort in dress, is not a blanket and a smearing of grease and red clay.

The clay now chiefly used is red ochre imported from England, and sold in small trading shops on the frontier. It is surely a distinct advance and a good result of education—good for merchants and manufacturers as well—when a native African leaves off a suit mostly of red ochre and grease, and appears in a suit of drill or duck, or even dark tweed on Sundays. The advertisements in the *Imvo Zabantsundu*, such as *isuti zamadoda* (men's suits) from 15s. to 20s.; and *ibatyi nebulukwe* (coats and trousers) from 17s. to 20s.; *ikaliko iprinti ezisand' ukufika* (calicoes and prints lately received) from 3d. to 9d. per yard, are not addressed to men and women who cannot read, and who still wear the red blanket, picturesque though it really looks. Such advertisements appearing every week in the native newspaper indicate the progress made, and they vary from ploughs to patent medicines and vegetable seeds, births, marriages, and deaths.

Varied and flexible as the Kaffir language is, it cannot meet all the exigencies of terms for manufactured goods, and of the above words only four are pure Kaffir. *Ikaliko,* and some other words, can be easily traced to their English origin.

CHAPTER IV

BENEFACTORS OF LOVEDALE—ITS NEEDS

HIS account would be incomplete without some reference to several large-hearted and generous donors who have been to some extent the makers of Lovedale, so far at least as the element of material aid is concerned. To these must also be added, though no roll of actual names is given, the long list of devoted men and women who have been my colleagues and assistants in the work of building up that place into its present state of comparative efficiency and strength. They also have been the makers of Lovedale. Some have toiled through the whole day; and others died at their posts ere the sun went down; and a few have taken part for shorter periods of service.

To many it may seem as if the work itself was uninteresting, unromantic, and irksome. It need not be so regarded, and in reality it is not. Moral wastes and spiritual desert places are like material wastes which have been converted into smiling fields or prosperous cities. They are only changed by a great deal of commonplace and unexciting work. The larger portion, and the most useful part of the world's work, is entirely unromantic. And African missionary work in some of its details is no exception—even though Africa is the land of romance—unless we let fall on it the glorified light of an entirely different future. And that is just what we labour for—a day in the future when the Dark Continent shall be a continent of light and progress, of cities and civilisation and Christianity. There is no good reason to doubt the coming of such a day.

But this portion of the narrative is intended to deal with the givers of material help. While we are grateful for the smallest contributions, it is only when considerable gifts reach us that any appreciable effect is produced on the finance of the year, or that buildings and other necessary works can be carried through. Without the aid given by some of those friends of the Mission, whose names are given below, Lovedale would not be what it is to-day.

These gifts have ranged during the past twenty years from £500 to £5000—the first donor mentioned below having given that amount unsolicited during his lifetime. With a few exceptions these amounts have come from men directly connected with South Africa, all of whom are well acquainted with the working of Lovedale, and most of whom had been more than once in the place and seen for themselves.

At the head of the list of benefactors stands the name of the late Mr. D. P. Wood of London and Natal. During his life he would only allow his gift of £5000 to be acknowledged as from a friend of the mission. Mr. Wood's maxim seemed to be that of the worthy old Quaker who said : ' I am to pass through the world only once. Let me do all the good I can, and with as little ado as possible.' After him comes Mr. John Stephen of Domira, Glasgow, who, in addition to many large gifts, also purchased the old British Residency of Block Drift, with the land attached, for £1000, and gave it to the Institution. The late Mr. James White of Overtoun, and Lord Overtoun following in his father's footsteps of generous support to missionary effort, have both also largely aided in the development of the place. This, however, is but a small part of all the munificent help given by both father and son to philanthropic and missionary work. The late Mr. John J. Irvine of King William's Town was from first to last a warm friend of Lovedale, and his bequest carried us through a period of financial difficulty. Mr. John S. Templeton of Glasgow, and Mr. John Usher of Norton, have also given generous unsolicited aid. Latest, though not least, is Mr. William Dunn, M.P. for Paisley, who has been a generous benefactor and friend of the Institution. Amongst bequests must be mentioned that of the late Mr. Macleroy of Port Elizabeth, and a sum to found a bursary by a native woman, who lived long at Lovedale, and who settled down in her declining years under the shadow of the place, in a small house built for her use.

Yet with the constant development of Lovedale, these sums, large though some of them were, only met the necessities of the time. There is neither reserve fund nor working capital to carry on the industrial work— and the absence of these causes constant anxiety and limitation of effort.

The cost of the numerous buildings alone amounts to over £35,000. Lovedale is in reality a small village.

There are many whom God has blessed with wealth, and who hold it chiefly as a trust, regarding themselves as His stewards rather than as absolute owners. This is the true view, since wealth is of value in this life only. Each day is steadily carrying all those who have it, as well as those who have it not, into 'a land where gold has no value, and luxury no meaning or use.' Those who give largely, are those who have acquired the power of giving. Some lose that power in proportion as their wealth increases; and many never possess it. As an unused power, it becomes dormant or dies altogether. Some at times find a difficulty in selecting objects that commend themselves to their judgments and sympathies, even though there are always applicants enough.

If these pages bring the wants of Lovedale before some of the supporters of missions, mainly, of course, within our own church—a good end will be served. Aid of this kind to Lovedale is much needed. The smallest gifts as well as the largest will be gratefully received. The largest gifts will not be too large for a place capable of far greater development; and such development does not mean selfish concentration on itself. It has not been so in the past, for other missions not less than Blythswood have drawn largely on Lovedale time and energy, money and men, and even life. After ten years of faithful service as an evangelist at Livingstonia, William Koyi found a final resting-place among the Angoni for whom he laboured; and further south, at the old station, S. Ngunana found an early grave after a shorter period of work. Both lost their lives, along with other brave and devoted men of our own race, in the attempt to plant the Gospel on the shores of Lake Nyassa. A similar instance occurred in connection with the more recently formed East African Scottish Mission. A further reason why aid may well be given, is that the sum allowed by the Foreign Missions Committee of the Free Church of Scotland does not wholly meet the salaries of the evangelistic and educational staff; while the industrial section receives no allowance whatever.

CHAPTER V

SOME GENERAL QUESTIONS

THE NATURAL INDOLENCE OF THE AFRICAN

OO much has been said, and received with unquestioning credence, about the unconquerable laziness of the African. He is like men of all other colours. He can, with patience, be taught to work. Where sufficient inducement is offered, and the new wants which civilisation brings act as a stimulus, he is willing to work. It is those untouched by education who can afford to be idle, and who are most markedly so. The heathen native needs no other clothes than a blanket, and lives on grain and milk. He naturally asks why he should work, when he has enough to live on. But he does work when taught to do so.

This view is not a missionary theory. It is simply another form of the following facts. All the transport of the country by wagons, and the rough work on farms ; the care of sheep and cattle ; the loading and unloading of all the ships which enter and leave the ports ; the rough work connected with the construction of now nearly 2000 miles of railway ; the working of the Kimberley diamond mines, and of the Johannesburg gold mines, has all been in the past, and is now carried on by native labour. In Central Africa the entire transport of all goods that pass in and out of that vast region is done by native porters, carrying on their heads, day by day for months together, loads up to 70 lbs. That *all* natives are willing to work is not true. Till civilisation or the Gospel comes they have no inducement or stimulus, either moral or material. The question is not, however, about the conditions of life in their wild state. It is whether they can be taught to work. That the African works as steadily as the European, it would be foolish to maintain. That he cannot be got to do a large amount of really useful work under proper training it is equally foolish to assert—though the assertion is constantly made, possibly often from want of thought, rather than want of heart.

QUALITY AND CHARACTERISTICS OF NATIVE WORK

Except in the case of a few who have enjoyed the advantage of long training—though not longer than that necessary to make a good European clerk or artisan—the quality of native work is not high. European supervision and constant direction are necessary ; but with these, *if considerable time* be allowed, fairly good work can be produced. Yet the average result, if the whole process is left to the natives, shows a want of exactness in measurements and the absence of thoroughness and taste. It would be surprising if it were otherwise. It is hardly to be expected that a people just emerging from barbarism, to most of whom the production of a straight line is a difficulty, and a perfectly true rectangle in wood or iron is an elaborate work of art, should, after a few years' training, turn out remarkably intelligent and efficient mechanics. But as compositors in printing, or in any work involving mechanical repetition, they make fairly good workmen.

EFFECT ON THE LABOUR SUPPLY

Dissatisfaction is sometimes expressed that we do not send out agents in much greater numbers, and of many different kinds, from evangelists, pastors, teachers, and printers, down to domestic servants. Though the numbers sent out are considerable, they can as yet have little effect on the labour supply of an entire country. What has been done shows what might be accomplished if the country itself, rather than a few missionaries, were to undertake the duty of industrial education on a scale adequate to its requirements.

It is not the proper work of missionaries, nor of the Societies which support them, to attend to the question of labour supply. Large as the staff at Lovedale is, it would need to be much larger if a Registry or Bureau of Native Labour, skilled or unskilled, were to be added. Such work, and all relating to the difficulties connected with the labour supply, belong to the Government or to the country to settle—if they can. That question is simply a portion of a very difficult problem, that of Capital and Labour. It troubles more countries to-day than South Africa.

IS THE RAW NATIVE THEN, NOT PREFERRABLE TO THE EDUCATED NATIVE?

Many answer this question always and easily in one way, and, of course, in the affirmative. If we were asked we also should give an answer, and say—

That for some kinds of work the raw native is as good, perhaps better, than his educated brother. For sheep and cattle herding, the raw native—in whom no desires after a better-paid occupation or a higher kind of life have been awakened—will probably attend more carefully to his humble duties than one who has received some education. In his uncultured state the thoughts of the native are about animals, their ways, and marks, and other peculiarities. Cattle to him are a valuable and pleasing kind of property. The pleasure he has in looking at fat cattle is second only to that of eating them, whether they are his own, or his neighbour's taken by mistake. He has different words in his own language for cows and oxen with slight peculiarities of colour, or dapplings of skin, which would never strike a white man, whose faculties are much more reflective, and less perceptive on such matters at least. The raw native will, if he makes his master's interest his own, more quickly notice if any of his herd are strayed or sick. He can do his work without any education, though for most other occupations he would be useless. The question of native education, and of missionary teaching generally, is surely not to be seriously argued on such points.

It is to be hoped also that no one who reads this will pervert the answer now given, into an admission that the raw native is better than one whose mental faculties have been awakened and sharpened by school instruction and manual work.

Is the Heathen Native Better than the Christian Native?

That he is so, is the singular opinion frequently expressed by travellers as to the results of missionary work in Africa, as well as in India, the South Seas, and elsewhere. In inquiring whether the heathen native is better than the Christian, we must, when a comparison is made, be sure that we have really a Christian native, and not a mere pretender. We must not call a black man a Christian simply because he wears clothes and goes occasionally to church. We do not make this classification even with men of a different colour of skin, in lands not so far away as India or Africa.

If we have genuine native representatives of both, the real Christian and the heathen, and their dispositions are fairly equal—that is, if there is no unhappy twist about the disposition of the Christian, making him a troublesome man to deal with—there can hardly be much doubt as to what the judgment of enlightened Christian opinion will be. In natural disposition the heathen may be a better man than the Christian ; more easy to get on with, and more faithful and conscientious. We sometimes prefer and employ a man for his acquired habits and powers got through education, though we may not like his disposition. But that is not the question under consideration. If any one, however, prefers Heathenism to Christianity, either in the concrete or the abstract, the argument may be regarded as at an end.

RELAPSES INTO HEATHENISM

This going back to the former life, in which the last state of the man is worse than the first, is supposed to be the opprobrium of missionary work, and the standing proof of its want of genuineness and solidity. It is constantly referred to in books of travel, when the writer has picked up a few current and untested opinions, transferred them to his journal, and produced them in his book when it appears. Many of these statements taken as general truths about missionary work are nothing better than travellers' tales. They are like the stories of the ostrich hiding its head in the sand when pursued, or the flowering of the aloe once in a hundred years ere it dies down. The ostrich is at best not a very wise bird, is sometimes rather vicious, but never so stupid as to do that. And at Lovedale we have miles of aloes forming fences, some of which flower each year, though they were only planted fifteen or twenty years ago.

This erroneous opinion about frequent relapses is due to two causes. First, to the belief that the number of those who go back to heathenism is much greater than it is in reality ; and second, it is commonly assumed that those who have so gone back, have been real Christians. But every native who wears clothes for a time, or comes to church as a pleasant variation in spending the Sunday, does not thereby become a Christian, meaning by that a converted man. He is perhaps not even a professed Christian—that is, a member of the church he occasionally attends.

But let us be fair to objectors. If it is said that many of those who become Christians fall again into *some* of the old ways of heathenism, nothing can be done except to admit the truth of the charge. This has always been the grief and discouragement of missionaries. The records of most native churches all the world over, so far as their membership is concerned, show that there is good cause for such sorrow. But it has been so from the beginning, even in the earliest churches planted by the Apostle Paul. What we have here, however, is not a proof of the absence of genuineness in missionary work, but a proof of the constant downward moral tendency of human nature, even with the aid and stimulus of Christianity. Yet despite of all this, from the earliest times till now, Christianity has thriven, and continues to spread. It is also certain to do so more markedly in the future, and to continue to be what it has been—the most important factor in the world's affairs, and in the evolution of mankind. All things now are explained by evolution, but an explanation which leaves out the main factor, as is so often done by the apostles of that doctrine, is likely not only to be incomplete, but entirely fallacious. And on the less evolved African of to-day, as well as on his more highly-developed brother in more favoured lands, there is no more potent influence in drawing him upwards, in evolving all that is best in him, than the religion of Jesus Christ, when genuinely received. This subject is further referred to in another chapter.

The Truth on these Objections

Our readers may rest assured that the objection to missionary work drawn from alleged relapses into heathenism, is, in actual fact, as ill-grounded as it is common in the opinion of many. It is common mostly amongst those who have heard of such work, but never taken the trouble to really examine it. Here is one opinion from a comparatively recent book, *Through the British Empire*, by Baron Hübner : [1]—'It is no rare thing to see pupils, who have scarcely left the excellent Protestant Institute at Lovedale, relapse into savagery, forget, for want of practice, all that they have been taught, and scoff at the missionaries.' The genial writer of these two volumes drove past Lovedale one day at the distance of less than two miles ; heard something perhaps from his travelling companion on this important question ; and yet here we have it in a generalised form—set forth by a man, travelled and cultured, acquainted with European diplomacy, and at one time an ambassador in a foreign court, as an opinion on the results of missionary work.

[1] *Through the British Empire*, by Baron Hübner. John Murray, London, 1886.

It would not be true to say that such relapses do not occur. They do occur. We know such, both by name and history. But the lurking fallacy lies in the indefiniteness of the statement as to the actual number, and the assumption that such is a fair conclusion as a general opinion on the results of missionary work. That conclusion every faithful missionary knows to be absolutely false, and is thankful to God that it is so. And a careful scrutiny of several thousand names has led us to the conclusion that the number is comparatively small. We have not been able to trace this result to beyond four to five per cent. of the whole number. This does not mean, of course, that the remainder have been exemplary Christians. The cases of men falling back for a time, longer or shorter, into some of the sins of heathenism is one thing; their relapsing into open heathenism and remaining there, as a general result of missionary work, which is the point really under dispute, is quite another. The former we in common with missionaries all over the world must sorrowfully admit as existing now, just as it has always done among all races and in all countries, since Christianity began to be preached.

CAUSES OF SLOW PROGRESS

Amongst the causes of the slow progress of the African and his present low condition, there must undoubtedly be reckoned the absence of religious beliefs, which means the absence of definite moral forces of the highest kind. The want of these, either in the individual or in a race, is a serious want, and has much to do with the mental vacuity and aimless indefinite life which characterise barbarism, to say nothing of its animalism and cruelty. If this be admitted, it will afford a complete justification of the missionary's method of work. His first and primary object is to implant true religion, and thus awaken the most powerful influence which exists for the guidance and elevation of the individual soul. The Bible is, therefore, his chief book, and spiritual results his best results.

But there are other causes of the slow progress of Christian missions in heathen lands than those which belong to the defects of the missionary or his method, and the unwillingness of the black man to leave his old ways of life and his old religion. Those who have visited any one of the mission fields of the world, and who have stayed long enough to become closely acquainted with what actually goes on there, will have no difficulty in finding one constantly recurring cause of a very serious kind. It is the kind of Christianity or no Christianity at all, which appears in the lives of some European residents who may come much into contact with the natives, or are actually settled among them. This holds equally good of India, Africa, and the South Seas. Perhaps the latter region is more cursed with a certain class of white men than either India or Africa. Such lives are amongst some of the most formidable obstacles to the progress of Christianity in the lands of heathendom. It is not necessary that a man be openly and flagrantly immoral. As native news and conversation are everywhere largely personal, it is true what Livingstone says—That amongst natives a white man's character and reputation are as well known as if he walked through the village in broad daylight, with the whole story written on his back.

Heredity and custom—that powerful unwritten law of heathen life, have also much to do with the slow progress which is made by a people passing out of barbarism into civilisation. We cannot expect those on whom the adverse influences of a thousand years are now telling, to advance at the rate at which other more favoured races are advancing. And, leaving divine influence out of account, we perhaps anticipate too much if we expect the people of any heathen country to fall at once into our ways and adopt our civilisation and Christianity simply on our recommendation. Human nature, fortunately or unfortunately, whether for good or evil, is more stable; and we must accept the facts of human nature as they are.

WATERFALL, CHUMIE RIVER

CHAPTER VI

OTHER INSTITUTIONS ON THE SAME LINES

OR a long time Lovedale has held on through good report and bad report, sometimes through more of the latter than the former, following these different but convergent lines of training. It has had to pass through a good deal of storm and stress, chiefly financial. Its work also has been three times interrupted by Kaffir wars. On two occasions the buildings were occupied by troops as a point of defence; the third time, in 1878, only as a place for refugees. These wars may now be regarded as things of the past, so far as that region of South Africa is concerned.

Several similar places were started at the same time as Lovedale under the aid which was given by Sir George Grey, when Governor of the Cape Colony. It was impossible that Missionary Societies should undertake the cost of buildings and other necessary expenditure for commencing industrial work, and many years ago the sum of £3000 was given for buildings at Lovedale, while various sums were given to other missions for the same purpose. The experiment, for such it was then, went on for a number of years. Then came the time for the investigation of results by the Education Department of the Cape Colony through which the money had been supplied. The consequence was that at several places these industrial departments disappeared in a day, like ships foundered at sea. Lovedale, however, was able to hold steadily on its course.

For a long time the Lovedale method was viewed with a doubtful eye by Home Societies. It is still so regarded by many Societies who address themselves to other and more special forms of missionary work, such as the exclusively evangelistic. The mistake here is assuming that all mission fields are alike, and that the same method is suited to every field in all its details, and at every stage of its progress. It is also assumed, but wrongly, that the spiritual side of missionary work must suffer when industrial and educational processes are also followed out. This may happen, but not of any essential necessity.

Men's thoughts, however, are widening with the process of the missionary suns, and there are signs that this *Combined Method* is the right method, not only for a small locality, or for a single mission, but for the whole African Continent. Societies and Committees which have long been sceptical about this method, and about the lawfulness of employing funds which they regard as given strictly for evangelistic work or preaching, are now beginning to give the best kind of approval—namely, that of commencing similar efforts.

BLYTHSWOOD, LIVINGSTONIA, AND OTHER PLACES

The natives themselves also understand the value of such instruction. Among institutions which have been started on the same lines may be mentioned Blythswood, in the Transkei, distant about 150 miles from Lovedale. It may startle into incredulity some who read this to be informed that the native people of that region contributed the large sum of £4500 for buildings to form an institution of this kind. Three different subscriptions of £1500 each, were asked for and paid by them. No contribution of equal magnitude has ever been paid within an equal time by the natives of any part of the African Continent. The story of Blythswood, its first inception, and the efforts made to create it, belong to missionary romance, if there be any romance in the finance of such work. Its story cannot be told here, but a handsome stone building, with a successful history of recent years, now represents those three heaps of money of £1500 each, chiefly silver, which were given by the native people of the Transkei, and carried away at the time for safe keeping in one of the Colonial banks.

Livingstonia, on Lake Nyassa, one of the most successful missions of the present day, was planned and is also carried out on the same lines. And the most recently formed mission in Africa, the East African Scottish Mission, almost under the equator, and inland from Mombasa about 200 miles, is intended to be similarly developed. The United Presbyterian Board of Missions has also, last year, resolved to add to its work at Calabar, on the West Coast of Africa, an institution of the same practical kind. In South Africa, also, there are several places where missionary work is thus carried on. There is one excellent institution of the Church of England at Keiskamma Hoek, in Kaffraria, and another in Grahamstown. The French Protestant Mission in Basutoland—a mission the reality and excellence of whose work is worthy of all praise—has also resolved to add to its printing department at Morijah other divisions of industrial work, as money may be forthcoming. They have also a small industrial station in the south of Basutoland. No one will believe that the French missionaries in Basutoland are ever likely to sacrifice the spiritual for the secular in their efforts. No one who reads this statement need have any fear that industrial work following upon that of education, and supplementing it, in addition to constant preaching, will anywhere do any harm. It will only do good, so long as the Gospel of Jesus Christ is the life and soul of all the teaching given, the inspiration of the entire effort, and is retained as the keystone of the arch to give stability, permanence, and utility to the whole.

A WARM MORNING IN THE GARDEN.

CHAPTER VII

OTHER VIEWS—LAY AND MISSIONARY

Opinions from Uganda

ACKAY of Uganda was one of the noblest of the many missionary heroes who have sacrificed life itself, in the attempt to carry the Gospel into the dense darkness of Africa. His latest views, and the final conclusion to which he came on the methods by which missionary operations in Africa at least should be conducted, are expressed in the last communication he sent for publication to the Committee of the Church Missionary Society. That communication he did not live to finish. It deals with the question of the means to be employed for the evangelisation of Africa. He starts from the point of fourteen years' experience and comparison of different modes of working. In a letter to his friend, the Rev. E. P. Ashe, he says :—
' I feel strongly inclined to throw up the whole matter on its present footing, and try a radically new plan.' And Mr. Ashe adds : 'Fourteen years of toil, and fever, and contradiction, and sorrow, and repeated disappointment, and he is strongly inclined not to shake the dust off his feet, not to return to England, but to try a radically new plan.'

What this plan was is fully developed in Chapter xvi. of his *Life*, beginning at page 445, and is given as an answer to the question, 'How is Africa to be evangelised?' No more important chapter on the work itself, and the means to be employed in African Missions, has been written in the present century.

Africa can never be evangelised by white men, nor can the rough work of laying the foundation of a new civilisation be done by them. Climate, language, number of men required, and the inevitable expenditure of vast sums of money, are all against the hope of that work ever being so effected.

White men can but direct and train the agents. On the character, quality, and method of that training, and on the number of men produced, depends, so far, the solution of that vast problem. The means or method to be employed should therefore be well considered.

His biographer states that Mackay latterly had ' strong convictions that the plan of working only by single or detached missionary stations at great distances inland, without a strong base on the coast, with occasional stations on the way, was a serious mistake of judgment, and would entail enormous expense and unnecessary loss of life. His mind lately seems to have fixed itself upon a plan of work not altogether untried, but capable of considerable expansion and adaptation to the supply of the needs of Africa.'

That was to plant strong central stations in healthy positions, and to keep them well manned and sufficiently supported, and to utilise the principles and methods of the Normal School for the thorough training of a number of carefully chosen natives of both sexes ; the training to be partly industrial, but chiefly educational and spiritual.

He arrives at his conclusion by a careful array and induction of facts, and then illustrates his plan by his favourite science of engineering.

It is almost his last word on the subject nearest his heart, and is worthy of careful consideration. It is highly probable that the plan he recommends might be worked with great advantage in combination with other methods which experience has proved to be successful in Africa, and might lead to a very considerable increase in the number of faithful and efficient messengers of the cross.

At very considerable length in the remainder of that chapter Mackay himself discusses what he calls 'The Solution of the African Problem.' He gives it as his belief, that the missionary fervour of the Christian Church is now being thoroughly roused, and states with a kind of regret ' that hitherto the methods of working have been a kind of chaos of vague generalisations lying dormant in the minds of Christian millions, but that now these vague views are being transformed into what may be called the Science and Art of Missions.'

With unquestionable accuracy he shows that all true progress in real knowledge, and the power to apply it practically, dates from the day when men began closely to observe and carefully to weigh and measure facts, and also to investigate those eternal principles ordained by God, which regulate or affect these facts. He shows further that the rate of such progress since then has been marvellous ; and that all success has been in proportion to the closeness with which men have adhered to the connection between these facts and those principles. In this he is but summarising the history of the inductive method, and attempting to apply it to the problem in question. As affecting Africa, he deals with the facts of its present condition, its ignorance and degra· dation, its past history and cruel wrongs and untold miseries, and the efforts that have been made from time to time under the influence of philanthropic impulse or eager desire to repair past injuries, ' to do something' for that continent. That ' something to be done,' while its object has been clear enough, has not as to the method to be followed been always equally clear ; nor has the necessary persistence and determination been maintained. Hence the result of many undertakings, and the expenditure of vast sums of money and many lives, has been too frequently only partial successes or complete failures. Those who are acquainted with the early efforts of a generation ago, such as the two Niger expeditions, as well as some other efforts since then, will recognise the historical truth of his statements. The recall of the Livingstone expedition by the Foreign Office in 1863 is another instance of this vacillation of purpose and incompleteness of result, because success was not immediate. Even at first many missionary efforts in new African 'fields have suffered in precisely the same way. Though it must be said for the credit of missionary enterprise, that it seldom gives up a field it has once occupied. If it withdraws for a time, it is only to re-form its broken line and to advance again to the attack. He then refers to the causes of this want of adequate success, or, as has sometimes happened, of complete failure. In the larger schemes for Africa's regeneration, these he sets down as due to intermittent efforts, to half-hearted action, to want of determined national policy, and to the withdrawal of support of a public or government kind, whenever danger became imminent or success was not speedily apparent. The jealousy between European powers as affecting national action on a large scale for the civilisation of Africa has also acted injuriously. And in missionary work he finds some of the causes of failure in the 'foolish rejection of the resources of civilisation, and in the insufficient staff of men at so many missionary stations throughout the whole zone of tropical Africa.'

The fitness of the American negro to do the necessary work in a climate which has hitherto been so fatal to the European is next considered. He rejects the idea that the evangelisation of Africa will be effected mainly by men of the African race born in America. Neither can the needful agents come from India, whose teeming millions need their own small band of native evangelists as much as Africa does. His conclusion is, that if the continent is ever to be evangelised, it must be by Africans themselves, duly trained and properly qualified for the work, and that strong missionary centres, as training organisations, thoroughly equipped and fully manned, and giving as good an education as the African is capable of taking, along with smaller stations at intervals for preaching or evangelistic work, is the right method to follow in the solution of this problem.

He states and illustrates this by regarding the work to be done as a vast chasm to be bridged, and employs his favourite topic of illustration—namely, bridge-building. The pier principle, he says, is that hitherto adopted in Africa in mission work. Lines of stations had been planted, but too frequently in unhealthy centres, or too far removed from each other, and these, like piers with bad foundations, have frequently collapsed. Others have tried the suspension principle, but with no better success. A tower of strength has been built on each side of the mighty chasm, one at Free Town on the West Coast, the other at Frere Town on the East Coast, and strong links have been hung out from either side in the hope of uniting in the centre, but the span has proved too great for the structure.

Mackay's View and Illustration

'Africa for the African, and its regeneration by the African, is a familiar watchword, and one that merits attention and examination. But how is the African to impart instruction to his fellows until he first receives instruction himself? There can be no *evolution* without corresponding and previous *involution*. You can get nothing out of the African without first putting it into him. Every effect must have a cause, nor will water rise higher than its source. Merely to teach the African reading and writing, and the elements of religious and secular knowledge, will be to leave him as before—a hewer of wood and a drawer of water. We must provide the African with the highest

education we can, only on the basis of African peculiarities. Who is to do
this? For many years together, probably for a century at least, this must be
the work of the Anglo-Saxon. But how and where is this to be done? In
Africa itself. Do not Europeans die off there in almost every part of its
tropical zones? Are not our funds also low, and existing stations already too
insufficiently manned to be able to undertake the work of carefully training a
few in addition to our ordinary work of the elementary teaching of many?
The problem is difficult, and under the present *régime* insoluble. Perhaps,
however, we may look once more to engineering for a solution.

'To span the Firth of Forth with a railway bridge has long defied the
utmost skill of engineers. The water is too deep to render piers possible,
while the span is too great to render the suspension principle at all feasible.
Did they therefore entirely abandon the scheme? No. They adopted a
natural principle, perfect in conception and comparatively easy in execution ;
although the work is on so gigantic a scale that to compare it with the largest
existing bridge, is like comparing a grenadier guardsman with a new-born
infant. The principle is called the cantilever, which even the most un-
mechanical mind can understand at a glance. At each side of the Firth a
high tower is built. Each of these towers is like the upright stem of a
balance or the stem of a tree, for from each side of the tower an arm or
branch is built outwards, one to the right and one to the left. For every foot
in length that is added to the seaward side, a similar foot in length must be
added to the landward arm, so as to make the balance even. The seaward
arms on each side are, however, not continued till they meet, but stop short
when their extremities are several hundred feet from each other. To fill up
this gap an ordinary girder is placed, having its ends resting on the seaward
ends of the two cantilevers. In this marvellously simple way the mighty
chasm, one-third of a mile, is spanned, which could not be done on any other
known principle.'

HIS APPLICATION

'Let us adopt this principle by analogy as our solution of the African
problem. Instead of vainly struggling to perpetuate the method of feebly-
manned stations, each holding only precarious existence, and never able at

best to exert more than a local influence, let us select a few particularly healthy sites, on each of which we shall raise an institution for imparting a thorough education if even to only a few. But instead of drawing from the general fund for the support of such institutions, let each be planted on a base of a fund of its own, and for every man added to the staff abroad let there be secured among friends at home a guarantee of sufficient amount to support him. This is the land arm of the cantilever, the man in the field is the seaward arm. Each institution must be a model or Normal School, no one being admitted on the staff who has not been trained to teach. The pupils to receive not an elementary, but as high an education as it is in the power of their teachers to impart, only with the proviso that every pupil is to become a teacher himself. These institutions to be placed sufficiently far apart so as not to interfere with each other; while for Eastern Africa only one language —namely, Swahili—to be adopted in all. From these centres, each with its large staff of teachers, the students will go forth to labour among their countrymen, thus filling up the gap between the long arms of the cantilever. *Lovedale and Blythswood in South Africa I would mention as types* already successful in no ordinary degree.

'We cannot put new wine into old bottles. We must educate, and that thoroughly, those who will in time take our place in the Christianising of their own continent. To teach these African children to exercise their reason and their conscience, to think, to judge, is a work which must be done. It is not every one who will be able to take part in such a work. Everything like ideas of race superiority must be absent from the teacher's mind. He must be a master of method, and first of all be able to impart the knowledge he possesses. While provision is made for imparting a thoroughly good education, that must be pervaded in every part by a Christian spirit, and based on the Bible, which will be the leading text-book, and which all must learn without exception.

'In this way probably soon, but under our present system *never*, will the prophecy of Victor Hugo be fulfilled, that "the next century will make a man of the African."'

This paper for publication was marked to be continued, but no continuation ever appeared. Death too early laid its cold hand on that of the writer.

Mackay I never met, though I have been within a few hundred miles of

E

his field of labour, and where his grave now is. No letter ever passed between us, though by some error or oversight his application to join the Livingstonia Mission in 1875 was not accepted. Months afterwards I heard of that application. He was at the time in Germany, while I was in Africa. It was too late to remedy the mistake.

But that he in Uganda, within a comparatively short experience, should have excogitated a method so similar to that now pursued at Lovedale, and which we have been for so long painfully working out by many experiments and not a few failures, is at least a remarkable coincidence. Our readers must form their own conclusions. No partiality of friendship led to this coincidence, for such friendship did not exist. Nor apparently did any cause, other than his own experience and his consideration of the results of missionary work, lead him to write so strongly, and thus pour out his heart in entreaty to those who have the home management of the missionary enterprise.

It is this, as an addition or complement to the essential and indispensable work of preaching, or the purely evangelistic method, which we have been striving at Lovedale to work out for many years. It was begun there long before it forced itself so painfully on Mackay's attention. It is the same method modified by circumstances and growth. We cannot, for instance, at Lovedale, which he gives as a type, now apply fully the principle of selection of pupils and students, because all who desire education, and who are willing to pay for it, are received. We cannot reject them. But while this is a drawback, there is a corresponding gain. The natives of the country are being taught to support themselves, and to pay for their education and missionary teaching. Without their assistance and co-operation in manifold ways, in paying as well as preaching, the problem of the evangelisation of Africa can never be solved. The Christian public of the home country can never pay for that evangelisation. Nor can white men be found in numbers sufficient to carry it through. And throwing the burden on the native people so largely as has been done at Lovedale, and since then at Blythswood and elsewhere, is a distinct step in the direction of African self-regeneration. It . is also a relief to the much-enduring, constantly-contributing missionary public in the home country.

Lovedale has many defects. What we say is, that it is full of imperfections, but to these our poverty and not our will consents. The want of means to sufficiently develop the place in comparison with what it might be, and with the vast field over which its influence might extend, is in part at least the cause of our imperfections.

Mackay's opinion, however, has its value, whether generally accepted or not. It is the conclusion reached by one of the most remarkable missionaries of the present day. He adopted this view after an apostolic life, and an experience such as few missionaries pass through. His self-denial, courage, endurance, clearness of judgment, and the elevation of his whole missionary life, throw utterly into the shade the average self-denial which most missionaries have to practise. In comparison they are things scarcely worthy of notice. His death was 'an irreparable loss to the cause of African civilisation;' and the life of this 'St. Paul of Uganda' will yet be an inspiration to many, whose lot it may be to labour in the coming day of Africa's brighter, better, and happier future, when it shall be a Christian continent.

OTHER LAY OPINIONS—SIR GERALD PORTAL'S

This Introduction is in part a description of Lovedale and its aims; but it is also a plea for a method, believed to be specially applicable to missionary operations in Africa. The opinion of the writer, or of any single individual missionary, however, may be partial or prejudiced, and therefore unreliable. The evidence of laymen has also its own special value. They judge from a different and perhaps a more practical point of view than that of the missionary.

There was recently formed in Eastern Africa a mission on the same principles or plan of work as is followed at Lovedale. The subscribers to that effort asked me to undertake its establishment in the territories of the Imperial British East Africa Company. This enterprise was due to Sir William Mackinnon and several of his friends interested in missions, and the sum subscribed was £11,840. The mission was begun in 1891, and was settled on the Kibwezi river. If wisely managed and with the necessary patience, it has every prospect of a future full of blessing to the people of Ukambani, where the Gospel is as yet almost entirely unknown. It should also aid in the development of the country, though in a minor but real way.

The road begun by the mission has now been completed to Mombasa, a distance of nearly 200 miles.

As evidence of a non-missionary kind it may be useful to quote from the most recently published book on Africa.[1] Sir Gerald Portal thus records his views on missionary work, on the spirit and method in which the lessons of Christianity and civilisation are to be taught, as well as his impressions of the Kibwezi station :—

'On the 18th of January we struck into an excellent and well-kept road, some ten feet wide, along which the men stepped out bravely. It led us for three or four miles through a lovely park-like country, over a clear, murmuring stream, to the station of the Scottish Industrial Mission at Kibwezi, about 200 miles from the coast. The road had indeed been cleared some months before for nearly thirty miles, but all the rest of it had unfortunately been allowed to become so overgrown with bushes and long grass that the track is almost imperceptible. As we approached this Industrial Mission evidences of its work and beneficent influence were apparent on every side. Fields were being cultivated, the natives were at work, and, standing with confidence to see our caravan defile, shouted out cheery greetings to the men. This was a refreshing contrast to the conduct of the inhabitants of a village only two marches back, who had fled with every sign of panic at the sight of a white man ; and who, when with difficulty they were induced to come into the camp, poured out bitter complaints of the exactions, ill-treatment, and the violation of domicile, which they had suffered at the hands of travellers.

'At the Kibwezi Mission we were received with every possible kindness and hospitality, and a pleasant afternoon was spent in admiring the neatness of the gardens, the grass-built houses, the well-kept turf intersected by walks and hedges, and in noting with pleasure the trust and goodwill shown by the natives of neighbouring villages. Although this Industrial Mission had only recently been established in the country—scarcely a year before—the progress it had made in the affections of the people, and the general good it had already effected in the neighbourhood, were really remarkable. The founders are to be congratulated on the success of their enterprise, which bids fair, if well supported, to rival in well-doing its elder sister, the Lovedale Mission of Southern Africa.

[1] *The British Mission to Uganda in* 1893. By the late Sir Gerald Portal. Edwin Arnold, London, 1894.

'This establishment affords another proof, if such were needed, of the wisdom of introducing the true benefits of civilisation among natives, not in the time-honoured English fashion, with a Bible in one hand and a bottle of gin or a tower musket in the other, but by teaching simple, useful arts, or by inculcating an improved system of agriculture, the benefits of which, and the additional comforts thus acquired, are quickly noticed and appreciated by the imitative African. The ordinary African, by the way, is not half such a fool as he looks. He appreciates as much as any one the advantages of a warm blanket on chilly nights, or of an iron hoe to replace his wooden spud in digging his little field, and the man who can teach him how to earn these luxuries will obtain a proportionate influence over him. But even in Africa the general laws of supply and demand are as strong as anywhere else. It is useless to offer the ordinary tribesman wages to serve as a caravan-porter, or as a coolie in some engineering work. The first he connects in his mind with heavy loads, sore and ulcerous shoulders, long marches, swearing headmen, and possibly a vision of a gang of poor fellows fastened together with chains ; the second means to him continuous work, more brutal headmen, and probably over all a terrible white man with a long stick, freely used, and strings of loud oaths in a strange tongue. After careful consideration, the African comes to the conclusion that whatever may be the inducements offered in beads, wire, or even blankets, this sort of thing is "not quite good enough." He hates regular hours or anything approaching to discipline, but he is quite ready to improve his own material comforts, and even to work with that object in view, if any one will show him what to do and how to do it ; but as the very foundation of his nature is suspicion, he must first have confidence in his teacher.

'I have no wish to be led here into an essay on the means of disseminating civilisation in Africa : the whole question is a most complicated one and full of difficulties, and it has already formed the subject of several thousands of pages from far abler pens than mine. Theories of the most admirable nature have been laid down and clearly expounded ; books, pamphlets, speeches, have proved to the world that the African native is a suffering martyr or that he is a demon incarnate, and treatment has been recommended accordingly. Africa cannot certainly complain of having received insufficient attention during the last few years, and yet it must be confessed that but little progress has been made, except in a few isolated instances. It is to be feared that the shortcoming has been in the practice of all the carefully-devised plans for the improvement of the lot of the negro. It is true that the long hide whip and chains of the white overseer are things of the past, and that slave caravans are now scarce, but it is to be greatly feared that the breechloader and the repeating rifles of the European officer and his half-disciplined troops are still emptied far too often in the cause of civilisation, and that the fire in which the African now finds himself is not much more comfortable than his former passive position in the frying-pan. All the theories, rules for guidance, and plans which have been evolved on this subject, are useless if the first principles are forgotten. The ordinary African native is a curious compound of suspicion, superstition, child-like simplicity, and mulish obstinacy. If he knows and trusts his leader he may be guided gently towards civilisation, may be made a useful member of society, and even a Christian, but he will resist with the whole force of his nature any attempt to kick him from behind into comfort or into heaven.'

The pith of this statement is not more happy than its absolute truth. Perhaps there has been a little too much preaching *at* the African, and too little patient teaching of him; too little appeal to the many-sided nature he possesses in common with all other men, despite of the common opinion that he is so degraded, lazy, and savage, that force is the only argument. The heavy stick or whip of hippopotamus-hide, with a place for a week or a month in the chain-gang of the caravan, is too frequently the chief method of teaching the African porter. This is often the only reward or result of helpless remonstrance, of some inability, or correction of some fault or offence, real or supposed. This chain-gang, I am sorry to state, is still an almost invariable accompaniment of East African caravans, even those led by Englishmen. It consists of a number, greater or less, of those regarded as refractory from any of the above causes, who march day by day, it may be for weeks, joined together by a long chain, one large ring of which is fastened round the neck of each of the unfortunates so dealt with. This method can be perfectly well done without, and with reasonable dealing there is ordinarily no necessity for it. I say this after actual trial. In the work of several caravans employed in the formation of the East African Scottish Mission no such means were used, even though the number of one of these caravans was over 270 men. On no account would I allow a missionary expedition to be graced or disgraced by the sight of ten or a dozen almost naked Africans marching through the country in chains, and under the blazing sun, carrying loads of 65 to 70 pounds on their heads. Through rough places, over steep gullies, and in winding thorny thickets, the torture must be terrible.

This explanation is necessary, as Sir Gerald Portal's reference to the whip and the chains of the white overseer being things of the past, apply not to caravans, but to plantation work; and regular slave caravans are now less frequent. The chain-gang in the East African caravans will probably be abolished by an order of the Imperial British East Africa Company, within their own territories at least.

A railway to Uganda or even half-way, would be an enterprise at once economic, strategic, and philanthropic.

KIBWEZI, EAST AFRICA—BUILDING MISSION STATION

CHAPTER VIII

THE ONE HOPE OF AFRICA

HE one hope for a better and happier future for Africa, and for its progress in true civilisation, is *viá* Christianity. If there is no hope this way, there is no hope any way, for the African continent. The same is equally true of the rest of the world, whether civilised or not. It is the moral element and not the material which forms the chief part of man's happiness and well-being, whatever be the colour of skin or the clime in which he dwells. We may indeed give the varied tribes of Africa's broad continent all the opportunities and advantages which the present century at its close has to offer. We may give them education and the knowledge of the advanced industrial arts of to-day. We may set up, as we are doing, civil administrations—at first very imperfect or incomplete, because of their expense and absence of revenue, and the distance they have to cover in those vast areas we call Spheres of Influence. But without another teaching, that of the Gospel of Jesus Christ, the hope of really changing African humanity is a vain and delusive hope. Without this there is ground for a ' reasonable despair for the future of the African.' But with this, unless all missionary testimony, and a good deal of lay testimony as well, is absolutely false, to say nothing of what Christianity has done for the civilised world, this despair is no longer reasonable.

Yet nothing but a moral and spiritual force, such as Christianity is, will either begin or continue the necessary change or produce those results, both permanent and progressive, which are essential to real success. Those outside changes and external reforms which civilisation and education bring, however excellent they may be in themselves, are not sufficient. They merely sweep and garnish the house and leave it empty. And the seven or more devils of civilisation which are ready to enter in, and will do so, are not much better than those of barbarism. They are less gross and savage, less cruel and bloody, but scarcely less malignant or wicked.

No better proof can be given than that afforded by the past history of the West Coast of Africa. Long before any West African missions were established, and for more than two centuries, ships went there, according to the old books of African travel, for gold dust. ivory, and beeswax. They took, however, in addition, cargoes of quite a different kind. Even before the end of the sixteenth century it was sound mercantile information in England that 'negroes from the coast of Guinea were good merchandise for traffic in the West Indies.' The straightforward commercial directness of this language, current among reputable merchants, who were also no doubt good Christians, disarms remark, but suggests the extent of the change between then and now. On that coast, the civilising influence of rum and the slave trade, of brass rods and blue calicoes, had for a long time a fair field, and even abundant and exclusive favour. What did this influence by itself produce to the unhappy people of that coast? Degradation of soul and body, exportation of the strength and labour of the country, and a social condition which may be fitly compared to the pestiferous malaria produced by the mud, mangroves, rank vegetation, and heat of those steaming rivers. The theory of improving the African anywhere, through all the wide area in which he dwells, by commerce or civilisation only, is a very surprising one. What is there in either the one or the other, by itself, to morally improve a savage, except to sharpen his wits and make him more cunning and overbearing, and supply him more abundantly with materials for a more animal kind of life? Civilisation, that 'complex entity,' so difficult to define, has to do with the present life. It is a 'gift of God' as well as a result of man's activity, and like all His other gifts, may be used by man for good or evil ; to rise higher or sink lower, according as it is accompanied or not by moral influence. But by itself for moral purposes, as every missionary knows, it is pointless and powerless ; and to primitive races by itself is a dangerous gift.

This view, that the one hope of Africa, and not less that of all other continents, lies in the religion of Jesus Christ, may seem to many a pious missionary reflection—merely that and nothing more. Let us escape from the limited view of missionary opinion into the wide horizon and clear air of modern Evolution. One of the latest and most advanced of its apostles has

F

done the world and modern science the very great service of calling attention to the importance of religion, not only as a factor in human progress, but as the absolutely dominating influence in race advancement.[1] Race qualities, as also factors in that progress, are admitted no doubt ; but a power is needed to turn these qualities to the best uses—the good of mankind rather than only and solely to the aggrandisement of a particular individual or race. And according to the quality of the religion, its moral purity, and the amount of truth it contains, so also has been its influence and power.

Taking the word *religion* in its widest sense, most, if not all mission-aries will agree with one of the fundamental statements of that work, that :

'In the religious beliefs of mankind we have not simply a class of phenomena peculiar to the childhood of the race. We have therein but the characteristic feature of our social evolution. These beliefs constitute the natural and inevitable complement of our reason. . . . They are apparently destined to grow with the growth, and develop with the development of society, while always preserving intact and unchangeable the one essential feature they all have in common in the ultra-rational sanction they provide for conduct. And lastly, as we understand how an ultra-rational sanction for the sacrifice of the interests of the indi-vidual to those of the social organism, has been a feature common to all religions, we see also why the conception of sacrifice has occupied such a central place in nearly all religious beliefs, and why the tendency of religion has always been to surround this principle with the most impressive and stupendous of sanctions.'

This is but an expression in scientific form of certain observed facts, and their application to a theory of man's history and progress. This is also the missionary's belief, experience, and hope. He has seen this factor at work. Under the influence of some of the lower forms of natural religion—it may be that of fetichism, or that of any other name or kind—the African is a very slightly evolved man, especially as compared with men of many other races. This black believer in his own natural religion of fear and grotesque faith, of dread of witchcraft, and strange practices to protect himself from its influence, is in consequence and at times rather an incomprehensible creature, and occasionally a very cruel one. But the missionary frequently sees him pass on to a belief in a higher and purer religion, namely, the revealed or super-natural religion we call Christianity. In the change or transit he passes from the level of a lower to that of a higher kind of man—so far as the rationality or humanity of his actions is concerned.

To bring about this change all influences except that of religion, even the strongest arguments and personal inducements, are entirely ineffective.

[1] *Social Evolution.* By Benjamin Kidd. London, Macmillan & Co., 1894.

He prefers his old savage life, with its absence of restraint, from clothes to morals, and its free indulgence, undiluted and unembittered by anything conscience may suggest. It is no argument to assert that certain social or personal advantages may have weighed with him. Generally the social results are disadvantageous, and even at times there may be persecution. Nor is it any mere restless desire for novelty that leads to such change. Despite the common platitude of missionary platforms about the heathen ' calling for the Gospel,'—they do not want it, and they are not calling for it.

Their condition is calling, but not themselves ; and the duty of Christians is calling on them to act. I never yet met an African who wanted to be troubled with the Gospel, till it began to trouble him. But when it does trouble him effectually, marvellous is the change it makes. It would delight the heart of the most thorough-going evolutionist of the school to which the now distinguished author of *Social Evolution* belongs, to see how the preferences and ' interests of the individual ' become subordinate to ' those of the social organism ' ; and how the antagonism between ' the inner and the outer life, the natural man and the spiritual man ' is reconciled when the new religion lays hold of the slightly-evolved primitive man. It all lies in this, that Christianity awoke the sleeping spiritual man. Or if the evolutionist, as necessary to his argument, will not concede that the spiritual man was sleeping, the new religion took him by the hand and led him out of a land of thick darkness, gloom, and horror—filled with malevolent shades and dreaded spectral powers—and brought him into the clear, sweet light of a simple belief in a God of goodness and love, such as Christianity reveals. It cannot be otherwise, since that religion comes from Him in whom is no darkness at all.

There is nothing new in this. It is a different statement of the old truth that the Gospel of Christ becomes the power of God unto salvation to every one that believeth, whatever be his colour or condition—white Caucasian or black African. All the radii of a circle, however vast, find both starting-point and terminus in its centre. And equally many of the perplexing facts in a wide area of human life, history, and varying condition, find an explanation in the power, effects, and existence of the religion of Jesus Christ—revealed though it is, and supernatural though it be. This dread—or, perhaps, more truly, this dislike—of the super- or supra-natural in religion is unreasonable ; and probably the day is not far distant when it will be deemed as equally un-scientific. It cannot be worthy of science to ignore palpable facts. Life is more than logic. Man is more than intellect. Brain is not all of him. And Reason's high function finds regions in man's life where its eye and its ear are powerless, and its processes are inapplicable and unworkable. There are human fears which may be called irrational, but that does not dissipate them. There are joys which may be called illogical, but that does not despoil them of their quality, their value, or their use. There are impressions and con-victions in man's spirit as fixed and immovable as the fundamental laws of thought. And the truth seems to be, that there is the impact—however ethereal it may be—of the supernatural world on man's life, and to exclude that element from his religion is neither wise nor practically possible. The savage man cannot do it, and the civilised man who tries it, only succeeds in a partial, dissatisfied sort of way; and he has to keep repeating to himself that he has done so, though he is doubtful all the while of his success.

Perhaps many or even most missionaries, if asked whether they accept all that is embraced within the two words 'Modern Evolution,' may hesitate before they add 'Amen.' They may even look with profoundest wonder at the upward steps by which the Ascent of Man is said to have been accom-plished ; and, if asked to assent, even the boldest may hold his breath for a time. The element of duration may also puzzle them. The evolutionist wants æons for his process. The missionary can do with less. In morals, as in mechanics, the intensity of the factor diminishes the necessity for time. The tremendous chasm between fetichism and Christianity is seen to be passed over at a single bound in the lifetime of the individual. The irrational conduct and cruel life of the former give place to the rational conduct and gentler life of the latter. The chasm between the two states was not bridged over by a slow evolutionary process built up of material influences and conditions, which in some perfectly unaccountable way assumed to themselves moral powers, and so transformed the man morally while elevating him from a lower to a higher material state. On the contrary, the change came with comparative suddenness, like the dawn in tropical lands. The orb of a new power shot up in the darkness of the previous life. And as men walk straight in the light, though they wander and grope in the darkness, the straight course of rational conduct forthwith proclaimed the enjoyment of a new day.

All missionaries have seen this transformation of life take place. And whatever they assent to, few or none will withhold their assent and testimony to the power of religion to effect changes in the individual, after all other forces have failed. And the multiplication of that influence has the same effect collectively, or in the language of the evolutionist, on the social organism. He seeks the laws which regulate that; the missionary seeks the men out of whom it is built up.

If all this be true the missionary needs no apology for his work. In the regeneration of Africa or of any heathen land, the truths he teaches are the main and indispensable factors. It is true he does not rest his belief on such reasoning. The foundations of his activity are the more fixed ones of personal experience, of generalisations from the world's past history, and first and last, the promises and purpose of God about this world and the men who dwell in it, as he believes and comprehends these declarations. But, so far, the missionary and the evolutionist, or some of them, are at one. The latter says that religious beliefs form the most powerful influences in the development of mankind. The missionary says that is true, that all his experience confirms this; and he further adds, that the truths of Christianity are the most effective, the purest, and the most beneficial in their influence, as well as the strongest and most permanent, when they really take root. And wishing the evolutionist success in his inquiries in the same excellent direction, and many more conclusions of the same kind, as at once scientifically true and practically useful, the missionary turns to his own proper work of trying to inculcate belief in these religious truths. All this paves the way for the appeal that is now to be made. It is not for African missions only. What applies to them applies to all.

CHAPTER IX

CONCLUSION AND APPEAL

APPLICATION OF THE ABOVE VIEW

TO make a new continent with different and better men in it, some influence is needed of a kind which, when once started, will be what may be called morally automatic. Or, to vary the illustration, a seed needs to be planted which will distribute and re-sow itself as time goes on. No other force but Christianity possesses this power. Either illustration will suit. For the seed of the kingdom of heaven tends to re-sow itself, and in the heart of the individual no truth is so self-acting as those truths which constitute the pure religion of Jesus Christ—when it is a reality in the heart. In all temptations, circumstances, and occasions of duty, it is there with its warning, advice, or prompting. Men and women are wanted to teach those truths. And no one can truly teach Christianity except those who themselves really know and possess it. Here, then, comes in the appeal and the necessity for Christian men and women to give themselves to such work, which is not merely that of preaching at stated times, however frequent, but of supplementing such preaching by the use of all those agencies and appliances which develop the intellectual and moral nature as well. The objection may be urged that such agents cannot become formal preachers of the Gospel. Every one in the home country who engages in Christian work is not a regularly ordained preacher. There are other ways of doing missionary work besides preaching.

Africans at first, and indeed at all stages, learn, as we all do, by what they see as well as by what they hear. Abstract truth, however comprehensive, does not tell on them. At first it is little better to them than the higher mathematics to a child. But the life and activity of the missionary agents tell wonderfully without much formal speech. And the mission station should be to them an object-lesson in order, progress, cleanliness, and industry, as well as religious teaching; and be also a place where they may be always sure of kind treatment. All this can only be accomplished by a variety of means, by much teaching which cannot find a place in formal preaching, and by other agents than the one or two paid agents, who form the regular staff of the mission specially devoted to such work. The latter class are inadequate in numbers, time, and energy. Hence the necessity for the existence of this new arm of the missionary service—a volunteer, or unpaid, or honorary contingent, whose work shall be less fixed than the statutory duty of the paid missionary—but scarcely less important as filling up the gaps, and giving it the firmness which belongs to all complete and well organised work. Hence the following Appeal.

APPEAL TO CHRISTIAN MEN AND WOMEN

There are in this country large numbers of highly, or at least well educated men and women—more of the latter than the former—who have means, and leisure, and sympathy with Christian work at home and missionary work abroad, and who yet have found no sphere for their energies. They have never thought of formally entering the missionary service as a profession, because they have no need to do so. For want of a definite invitation, or because they think no field exactly suits or requires them, or that there is no post they can fill, their missionary sympathy, personal energy, gifts, and education, lie comparatively unused, and life slips on till it is too late to take a new course. Yet in some instances, such as that of Miss Tucker, better known as A. L. O. E., the choice is sometimes made late in life. A similar instance is that of Mr. Monro, C.B., late Chief Commissioner of Police in London. Though he is what may be called an independent missionary—that is, is not formally associated with any Society, he yet acts in close and sympathetic connection with the Church Missionary Society in one of their fields of labour, Krishnagar in India. He also holds a position on the Calcutta Corresponding Committee, which is the local administrating body of that Mission in Bengal. There are others who have never regretted their decision or the step taken.

That there are many such ladies both in Great Britain and America cannot be doubted. They possess the wish to work, but the way is not open. The fault is not theirs, but that of their surroundings. A certain unwritten law circumscribes their energy and willingness to work. They have abundant leisure, are often 'weary of the rolling hours'; and sometimes 'know so ill to deal with time' that life becomes often more or less insipid.

There are also, though in smaller numbers, young men who have leisure and culture and enough to live on, and who also sometimes think life might be better spent in helping the spread of Christianity abroad, than in making a little more money, or merely amusing themselves at home. There is room and need for all such in the mission field. There are now, and have been a few such men and women so engaged in such mission work. The Hon. Ion Keith Falconer was one of them. He chose the blazing climate of Aden, or near it, and the not very inviting field of work among the Mohammedans of Sheikh Othman, in Southern Arabia. And I have met such cultivated women in Central Africa, at Zanzibar, in connection with the Universities' Mission, and also at other places. One well-known inland mission in China has been fortunate enough to attract a considerable number of such volunteers. The Church Missionary Society and the Society for the Propagation of the Gospel have also a considerable force of this kind. This excellent addition to the regular missionary staff is more common in English than in Scottish Missions, though it is not quite unknown among the latter. There are such ladies at the Blantyre Mission on the Shiré Hills, and at the Gordon Mission in Natal, founded by the family of Lord Aberdeen, as well as in those missions already mentioned.

But at Lovedale not one such labourer has as yet joined us, though before long it is possible there may be a few. Yet Lovedale is one of those places which offers the greatest variety of missionary work to those who are able and willing to do it. Any who has some gift he is willing to use for the cause of Christ, or can acquire some qualification to suit him for work, might find a sphere there. We could take twenty such workers, and find employment for all—the time and amount of work to be so fixed by those who offer. The only condition is that each man be able to do some one thing, and to be able to do it well; and be willing to communicate his knowledge to others, and observe fixed and regular hours of duty. By the addition of such volunteers the number now taught at Lovedale might be doubled. Its efficiency might be far more than doubled, and its influence made to extend over a wide region stretching northwards to the equator.

The chief argument for this volunteer service, in addition to what has already been stated, is that it not only increases the comparatively small force at work as yet in heathen lands—small when the population on which they act is taken into account, but it is the only way by which an adequate force can be raised and maintained. Frequent deficits indicate that missionary expenditure is always outgrowing income, and as a rule missionary committees are chronically impecunious. Yet there is a store of force in the shape of unutilised labour, largely lying unwrought at home, for want of invitation and organisation. It is like the unused force of our waterfalls from Niagara to the small streams of our Scottish hills, which is now being converted into mechanical power and light. For thousands of years that latent force has been running to waste. These streams, large and small, have delivered their tribute waters to the sea, and while doing so have blessed and beautified the lands through which they wander. But now their waste power is being turned to delightful and valuable uses. They are none the worse, and the dwellers on their banks are much the better—being greatly benefited and enriched. The gigantic scheme by which Niagara is now being turned to use will verify this illustration. But before this power can be so caught as it passes, skill and thought, and the intervention of the electrician with his subtle processes are needful, and the necessary mechanism has to be set up.

There is in the Christian church a similar force. It consists of genuine sympathy and interest in missions, and a willingness to work, which require skill and organisation to employ. It will take some time and some delicate work so to arrange and combine it. But what has been done in the case of the Salvation Army in home work—whether we approve of all its forms and methods or not—may be done for the mission work abroad.

The idea may seem to many Utopian and Quixotic. So also did the whole enterprise of missions at the beginning of this century when the 'consecrated cobbler' dreamt day and night about the conversion of India. There are gentle women and energetic men who might be so employed— only a few might be forthcoming at first, but more would follow after a time. Undoubtedly there is a class of such labourers existing. Its existence is due to the more practical forms in which the Christianity of our day is manifesting itself. And its representatives if they were asked—Why stand ye idle all the day? might say with justice—Because no man hath hired us! This, interpreted here, means, because no missionary committee hath invited or organised us. To all such who may be willing thus to serve Christ, there need be no hesitation in saying—Go or come ye also into the vineyard, by offering to go; and be sure of this, that whatsoever is right, that shall ye receive, when the day is done, which it will very soon be.

This form of service has the further value that it is a distinct advance in the idea of missions, as a duty of the individual, and not the business only of the church in its collective capacity or responsibility. It represents the best and highest form of giving. It is not merely the giving of one's money but of one's self—best expressed by the man who, when asked what he meant to give to the collection at a missionary meeting, said he meant to put himself into the plate. There is no fear that this auxiliary force will become too large to be employed. Yet the second century of Protestant Missions will not be very old before this force will be a very large one. It hardly needs to be a prophet to foresee that.

One or two hints or friendly cautions to any who may think of such work are all that is necessary. The first thing to make sure of,—is the motive. This is all-important, and though it may be in this case as in so much of human conduct, more or less mixed, yet if the main element exists, no one need go far wrong or feel much doubt. That motive is, and always should be, a sincere desire to obey Christ's last command, and pity for human souls to whom life must be a strange mystery, and death a very great darkness. Nothing else as a motive will do. Ambition is of no use. Religious restlessness will not be cured by a new field in another latitude. We change our skies, but not our minds, by sailing across the seas to missionary work or to any other occupation. Constitutional activity, mental or physical, will be of use, but not of the highest use without the power of the true motive. The native people everywhere recognise with an unerring instinct the missionary who is anxious for their good, because he loves and pities them, and who works for this end, rather than for the mere success or éclat of the work, because it is his. This latter end is a subtle temptation of the devil's own devising, and it dogs the steps of the missionary as steadily as his own shadow.

And as to qualifications, natural or acquired, not every one who thinks himself or herself qualified to become a missionary is so merely by the existence of such a wish or desire, or even by purity of motive. A trial for a few years and experience alone can decide that.

Another hint to all such, or any who offer, is this: Join some regularly established society, preferably that attached to the church with which you are connected, rather than new enterprises or less regularly constituted organisations. New enterprises require experienced men; and the main burden and responsibility of them should fall on the *regulars* of the missionary force—supplemented if absolutely necessary by those who are volunteers, and who have their experience to gather. Do not be led away by missions or organisations promising a primitive simplicity and method in the work. There is no royal road to missionary success either individual or general, so far as human effort goes. A century of experience has taught many lessons to those regularly constituted societies which now direct the great work of the mission enterprise at home.

Some again, who cannot go as unpaid agents, are led to join missionary enterprises, and are misled by the idea of self-supporting missions. There are no such things in reality. The agents of all missions must be either of the class to whom this appeal is made, and who in God's providence have enough to live on without the necessity of working; or they belong to the class who have not such means, and who must, therefore, become the paid agents of some society if they are to become missionaries at all.

The best proof of the need and value of association or co-operation with some of these older societies may be given in a single sentence. It is this. *The bulk of the missionary work of the world has been, and is now being, done by the older and more regularly constituted societies.* They have each a history and a varied experience to guide them. They have also the constituency of a Christian Church behind them to give the necessary financial steadiness, and enable them to overcome temporary reverses. Separate or independent missions are valuable, but the others have done the work. I shall avoid taking instances from Presbyterian Missions, though such might be given. I might refer to the London Missionary Society, whose early efforts gave a great impulse to missionary work in the first half of this century, and which now covers an extensive field. There is also the still older Society for the Propagation of the Gospel, whose agents work with wonderful devotion, though there is less co-operation with other societies abroad than is desirable.

Instead, I shall take the largest of all, the Church Missionary Society. The stations of this noble society and splendid organisation girdle the globe and thrive in every climate. They stretch from the rigorous north-west of the American Continent in Alaska to Sierra Leone and Yoruba in West Africa, and Uganda in the east; through Arabia and Persia and India, west, south, and north; through China, Japan, and New Zealand. The methods of this society embody a great variety of forms of work, yet they chiefly run on the great trunk line of missionary effort—preaching or evangelistic work, with more or less educational work in addition, in most of its fields. It is impossible to study the work of this vast organisation,—which controls the expenditure of a quarter million sterling annually, with a correspondingly large force of agents, European and native, of many climes, colours, and nationalities,—without admiration; and without the prayer, that God may further bless its efforts for the coming of Christ's kingdom on this earth.

So varied are now the fields of missionary work, that it is possible to choose almost the degree of latitude as well as the people, among whom one wishes to labour, though the greater portion of that field lies within the tropics. Even in Africa there are to be found regions with the finest climates, as well as others with the worst or deadliest in the world. The former lie in the south and north, and the latter on the west coast and in the low valleys of the great rivers, though experience is lessening the dangers of residence even in these valleys.

Nothing in the above appeal is to be construed into the view or notion that any one is fitted to become a missionary to the heathen, simply because he has a strong desire and a pure motive. Perhaps there has been a tendency amongst more than one of the independent missions, to familiarise the mind of the English people with this false idea. It is a pity to keep any one back who is anxious to go abroad to aid in the spread of Christianity—the one great remedy for the world's ills. But the conditions of missionary service are less simple than they were; and every year they are becoming less so. The principle of division of labour is being more and more applied; and a man must be thoroughly competent in some one direction to be an efficient worker. The day has gone by when it was thought any one was qualified to be an African missionary if he was a sincere Christian and could trundle a wheelbarrow. God works by the humblest instruments in the two kingdoms both of nature and grace; but the humblest instruments do not mean the least fitted. Among the silent forces of nature the most potent are often the least obtrusive. And in the higher kingdom the question is simply one of personal influence—the possession or not—of that subtle power which acts on others spiritually or intellectually. Humble men often possess this spiritual force. The range of its influence is dependent, so far, on the possession of other qualifications mental and physical, fitting the man for the work he has chosen. His success as a missionary will be in proportion to the amount of moral force he carries with him or within him.

Should any one who may read this choose the African continent as a field of work, he need not fear that his life's work will be labour lost. There can be no doubt about the future of that continent. Long the least known and the least developed, the most neglected and the most despised of all the continents, dark Africa has suddenly emerged into the light of day. And the time is not very far distant when it will be a great field of human enterprise and activity. The scramble among nearly all the great European Powers to obtain the largest area of that hitherto neglected land, means belief in the future of the African continent.

Similarly the day is coming, when the common opinion about the African will be as completely reversed, as has been the opinion of the civilised world about the continent in which he dwells. Long degraded and despised, and regarded for countless centuries as only fit to be a chattel and a slave, there is that in him, undeveloped though it be, which will yet make the African a man amongst other men—able to hold his place and do his work in the world. Individual tribes and sections of races may disappear, as has happened amongst other nations and races. But about the African race as a whole, there is a vitality of a remarkable kind, even though it is as yet only or mostly a physical vitality. Yet that is the basis of all higher activity. Developed thought and feeling rest on sound physical health and power.

The population of Africa will steadily increase now that the slave-trade is doomed, and all civilised nations have formally at least washed their hands of that great iniquity. The evil, however, still exists and is carried on in a stealthy way, chiefly on the east coast by Arab traders, and especially at Zanzibar. In the African continent, wherever its people can enjoy a few years of peace, its desert places again become filled with life. The villages raided and burnt by slavers, and out of which a few terror-stricken fugitives escaped with nothing but bare life, are again rebuilt; the fields are cultivated, and the village becomes noisy with the life and play of children. The wonder is that the whole African continent has not long since become depopulated. For almost numberless centuries, its central areas at least, have been the slave-hunting grounds of the world. Christians, Mohammedans, and Pagans have been alike guilty—so slowly does the general or national conscience grow. To each and all the three, the African had for all these centuries looked in vain for one glance of human pity, or one movement of human help and sympathy. But these bad days are now over, or nearly over. And it is part of the glory and honour of Christ's religion that its truths and its spirit have banished this evil business from the trade of the civilised and Christian world. But for the spirit and power of that religion, the evil thing would have been in existence still.

The African is deserving of better treatment. He has his faults as men of all races have, but he shows a docility, affection, and loyalty to the white man when he is thoroughly trusted, scarcely shown by any other race at the same social level. His trust in the white man's rectitude and power is absolute, until he is rudely undeceived, as he has been ten thousand times, by some startling disclosure of the absence of that rectitude; and then though the idol may retain his power, he is a fallen idol, to be feared but not loved. Can we wonder at his suspicion and distrust? According to some the African is vindictive, which is absolutely untrue as a quality of the race; at least in comparison with many other races. He is regarded as a liar and a thief, and as destitute of moral instincts. It would be curious to hear an African on these charges in the light of the slave-trade and its history; or to hear his opinions on the doings of many white men in much more recent times than the days when full cargoes of slaves were run from both sides of the continent.

O my countrymen, and men of other civilised countries as well—more favoured and blessed than that unhappy continent—how badly we have used the great gifts and powers God has bestowed upon us in our dealings with Africa and its people! How ruthlessly have many portions of that continent been laid open by some who have traversed those regions for the first time ! Our own countrymen, with all their faults, have not been the only or the greatest sinners in this matter. How poorly even at the best have we discharged the great duties God has laid upon us in virtue of the gifts He has bestowed! Still, in God's time, apparently a better day is coming, for clearly ' O'er that weird continent morning is slowly breaking.'

We return again in a final word to the one power and influence sufficient for the regeneration of Africa. It has been the keynote through all these pages. That one force is the religion of Jesus Christ, taught not merely by the white man's words, but what is far better, by his life, as showing the true spirit of that religion. Civilisation will also need to bring various forces, important and subsidiary ; but yet without the main factor, the problem will not be solved. Disappointment will be the only result, if the best and most potent element is left out. This is appeal and reason enough to all Christian men who can either go to Africa, or aid at home in the great work of its regeneration.

The coming King of this earth is Jesus Christ. He is the world's larger hope. The hope of a better and happier day does not lie in socialistic panaceas, or in dreams about equality in a world where no two men are, or remain equal for a single day, nor in the wholesale distribution of the hard-won fruits of honest industry among the lazy and dishonest. These are the remedies of a well-intentioned, but badly-instructed, and sometimes slightly crazy benevolence. These ill-regulated remedies only make matters worse. They are the falsehood of extremes, and the exaggerations of human thinking applied to those everlasting truths which fell from the lips of the Greatest Human Teacher. The little grain of truth they contain has been stolen from Christianity itself. A saner spirit, and a more robust common sense, and a sounder interpretation of what Christ has taught, and above all, the practice and the spirit of those teachings, must come first. That the law of His kingdom, love itself, will yet become universal law among men is the dream of poets and the hope of all Christians. It has been, and remains so, even in the face of spectral doubts, and the pain and perplexity of the constant facts of daily life,

No other power can bind men together.   That law is, in the world of spirits, what gravitation is in the world of matter.   Hence it is true—

> ' All things grow sweet in Him,
>   In Him all things are reconciled.
>   All fierce extremes
>   That beat along Time's shore
>   Like chidden waves grow mild,
>   And creep to kiss His feet.
>
>   Within His reign
>   Are no more tides that
>   Murmur and complain ;
>   Nor ancient foes that seem
>   Their life from out each other's
>   Hate to draw.   .   .   .'

He alone it is

> ' Who brings the fading flower of poor Humanity
>   To perfect blossoming and sweetest fruit.'

Many no doubt regard all this as a dream.   That cannot be helped. This truth will be the world's experience later on, when all experiments have been made with all other remedies, and all have been found empty, futile, and void.   One of the plainest and saddest facts of the present day, as the result of our justly boasted nineteenth century civilisation is, that individual happiness and general contentment are not keeping pace with modern progress. Man's heart, insatiable as the sea, needs something more.

MAIZE FIELD, LOVEDALE FARM—SANDILLIS KOP IN DISTANCE

FIFTY VIEWS FROM PHOTOGRAPHS

H

VIEW LOOKING SOUTH-WEST

THE immediate surroundings of Lovedale have been described in a previous page.
The above view shows only the roofs of two buildings and a portion of the Lovedale
lands, but it gives a fair representation of the contour of the surrounding country
on the south. Immediately to the north rise the Amatola mountains, with beautiful
fertile valleys and many streams. This country was the home of the various tribes
forming the true Kaffir race. Four times during the last sixty years they have
fought stubbornly with the British power for the possession and sovereignty of this
territory. The first great struggle occurred in 1835, and was very disastrous to the
Kaffirs in land, property, and life. Then occurred the War of the Axe in 1846.
This was followed by a protracted struggle in 1850-53 ; and finally by the war of
1877-78, in which Sandilli lost his life, having been killed by a rifle shot near
Pirie, thirty miles distant from Lovedale.

ROAD THROUGH LOVEDALE

THE above view shows a road passing through Lovedale, with the water-course which supplies the station with water. It is brought from the Chumie River, a distance of over two miles. This water-course was begun in the early days of the Mission, before the adjacent territory was annexed to the Colony, by Captain C. LENNOX STRETCH, then Diplomatic Agent with the native tribes. The work was carried through by him, in conjunction with the Mission, at a cost of over £600. One half of this was generously met by Captain Stretch himself, and the other half by the Mission, aided by the contributions of two members of the respected Society of Friends, who were travelling through South Africa, and who visited Lovedale while the work was going on.

Almost everywhere in Africa the natives give each European a name in their own language. If he does not know it, they can thus talk about him in his own presence. The name may be a title of respect or a nickname, in which the individual's appearance, manner, or even gait is very cleverly hit off. Captain Stretch was known by the honourable title of 'Xolilizwe,' Peacemaker in Land, or Improver of the Country.

MAIN APPROACH.

Good roads, and many of them, form a feature of Lovedale and its immediate surroundings. The making of these and keeping them in good order, later on, are part of the work of those in the ordinary school classes. The above view represents the main entrance into the place, which, when first occupied by the Mission, was merely unreclaimed land—in America, the prairie, in South Africa, the *veldt*.

Roads in Africa only come with civilisation. The whole continent is a vast network of narrow, zigzag footpaths, which generally involve at least one-fourth more of distance in traversing. With the white man comes the necessity for wheeled transport, and broad roads make their appearance. As the native pupils have to make these roads, we find this the best method of teaching road-making. Gradually it takes effect in the minds of a few of the most active and energetic. Not that any one attempts a road such as the above, nearly thirty feet wide, but at their own houses we find now and again a few straight paths, a few feet wide, cut where such were never cut before.

THE BEGINNING OF LOVEDALE

THIS building was the first humble beginning of Lovedale, the earliest permanent church. It was built of rough stone, with thatched roof, clay floor, and benches formed of yellow-wood slabs nailed to supports driven into the soil below. As indicating the progress of the station, it should be looked at in contrast with the next view.

This church, now utilised as a schoolroom for elementary classes, was used for more than twenty years by the first native congregation. Under its bare rafters many earnest addresses were given by the older missionaries. Many a curious congregation assembled within its walls. Instead of the well-dressed assemblage of worshippers which now meet in a better church, men and women came in skin karosses, the best dressed being well painted with red clay. Shortly they would get tired of those new things called chairs, and squat down on the floor. Their behaviour was generally decorous. At first they had but a vague comprehension of the new truths addressed to them. But when something which seemed very strange was spoken, or any unfortunate slip was made in the language, one with a smile would nudge his neighbour, as if to say, 'Listen to that—you!' The new truth made way for all that.

EDUCATIONAL BUILDING

THIS view represents the chief educational building at Lovedale, though there are several others also used for that purpose. That shown above is one hundred and seventy feet long, and is built of hard altered sandstone. It contains twelve large rooms, used as class-rooms, library, and book store; and also a large hall about seventy feet long, with a roof of fifty feet span. This hall is used for religious services, lectures, and general meetings. All except the stonework of this building was done by the Industrial Department of the Institution; and it is the largest of the kind used for missionary and educational purposes in South Africa. The buildings at Lovedale, including workshops and dwelling-houses, number twenty-five in all.

In contrast with the previous view, it tells of change and progress,—the old order changing and giving place to new. But the accommodation is all needed—and, as it is, is barely sufficient.

IN THE LIBRARY, LOVEDALE

THIS interior shows one of the rooms of the main educational building used as the library. It contains over 7000 volumes. One half is filled with recent books in general literature, and the other with older standard works, chiefly theological. The newer books come from Mudie's twice or three times a year. The library is supported by subscriptions, by an annual grant of thirty pounds from the Cape Government, and by a small endowment by the late Miss MORRISON of Glasgow.

The foundation of the library was made very many years ago by the gift of nearly 2000 volumes from friends of the Mission in Scotland. It has been more than once well weeded since then, and though not large, contains a much greater selection of really good books than can be found in the libraries of many colonial towns. All have free access, even the European residents of the district, on payment of a small annual subscription, which varies according to the number of volumes, from ten shillings upwards.

9 A.M.—WAITING FOR THE BELL

AT 9 A.M. the regular work in the school classes begins, though some classes meet as early as 7 A.M. A considerable crowd has collected, attracted by the doings of the photographer on the morning of his work at this spot. They are waiting till the bell sounds. On the left are several of the masters, some European young men, sons of missionaries, and others who are pupils, with two or three little creatures from what is known as the station or most elementary school. Some of the very young boys still come in the simplest form of civilised dress—a shirt, which is for many years their sole clothing. In some of the more distant villages, —a dressed sheep-skin, worn with the wool inside, is still the clothing of these small scholars. But when they advance to the classes of the Institution, civilised dress and attention to cleanliness is the rule which must be observed.

64

CLASS GROUP

THIS group contains theological students and others preparing as teachers of native schools. Some of the former are already at work as pastors of native churches. This class is under the care of the Rev. W. J. B. MOIR and the Rev. T. DURANT PHILIP. An effort was made some years ago to combine the two Presbyterian missions— that of the Free and the United Presbyterian Churches and that of the London Missionary Society—in theological and general education. This co-operation, it was thought, would secure strength, efficiency, and economy. The London Missionary Society has been worthily represented during the last seven years by the Rev. T. D. PHILIP, whose early labours at the old L. M. S. Station of Hankey and later at Graaf Reinet are well known. But this combined effort of all the three missions, even with these important objects in view, has unfortunately not been realised.

CLASS GROUP

AFTER three or four years in the school division and one year of training as teachers, nearly all endeavour to take a certificate of some kind from the Education Department of the Cape Government. The one chiefly sought is the Elementary Teachers' Certificate, which qualifies the holder for teaching the ordinary mission schools in native villages. For this they enter into competition and take the same examinations as Europeans at the same stage of advancement, and with the same object in view. As the work is all in English, with one paper in Kaffir or Sesuto for natives, obviously they compete under considerable disadvantage—from having to use what is to them a foreign language.

GENERAL GROUP IN FRONT OF MAIN BUILDING

THIS group shows the native residents, with the teaching and general staff. It is a very mixed group, with white faces here and there in the black mass, and includes Europeans, Kaffirs, Fingoes, Basutos, Barolongs, Zulus, and Tongas, and a few even from the Zambesi, the River Shiré, and Lake Nyassa. Those from the latter region are comparatively few, and have been sent down by their missionaries for education. But still natives come of their own accord from great and varying distances. An examination of those areas showed 350 coming from distances varying from 1 to 100 miles; 150 from distances varying from 200 to 500 miles; and a smaller number from 500 to 1000 miles, exclusive of the Gallas who come from a greater distance.

GENERAL GROUP A FEW YEARS LATER

THE above is similar to the foregoing but showing several changes on the staff, and an almost entire change on the great body of the natives. It is given as taken eight years later, to show the normal numbers—which are rather increased than diminished. The same remarks apply as to distance, variety of tribes, and the areas from which they come. There is a certain beneficial result in this diversity of area and distance. Amongst those who return to their homes, some may have become rather conceited, but there are always others who carry new and useful ideas with them. They also take a better position among their fellow-countrymen, and if there is any civilised employment where they go, they are more eligible for it. They also spread the desire for education and civilised ways. Some do a great deal better, they spread the teachings of Christianity wherever they go.

68

RESCUED GALLA SLAVES.

ABOUT four years ago H.M.S. 'Osprey,' commanded by Captain GISSING, captured on the East Coast of Africa a slave dhow containing over 200 slaves. The above view and another further on represent 64 of those so rescued. They are mostly Gallas, and come from Gallaland, close to the equator. As a race they are akin to the Somalis, and differ considerably from the tribes lying to the south.

A number of those so rescued were sent to the Keith Falconer Mission, near Aden, but the mortality among them was so great that it was necessary to remove them to a healthier position. They were brought to Lovedale by Dr. PATERSON in 1890, and are now supported by congregations and Christian friends in the home country. Later on, it is hoped, they may form the nucleus of a Christian mission and colony in their own country, which has, as yet, no mission, or they may join the East African Scottish Mission as native agents in different capacities.

L

KAFFIRS, FINGOES, AND ZULUS

To European eyes all black faces are quite indistinguishable at first, whether taken singly or in a mass. After a little, the same variety of expression and character appears as is seen in the countenances of men of other races.

The above group is formed on no other principle than that its individual members received some aid in their education from benefactors in the home country. They represent Kaffirs, Fingoes, and Zulus, and show the diversity referred to, with also diverse histories. One, as a child, was thrown away by his tribe in a small-pox scare, after the death of his parents. He was kept alive by his missionary for two months in the forest. Another went to St. Helena for some years as interpreter with the petty Zulu chiefs, who were banished to that island after Cetewayo's death. Another was a member of the first African Choir which visited this country four years ago, and which had the honour of performing before the Queen. That choir was a sorry business for the most of its members—resulting in the death of several, and the impoverishment of all. It was a heartless swindle, perpetrated at the black man's expense—Mr. STEAD and the support of the *Review of Reviews* notwithstanding.

1 P.M.—GRACE BEFORE DINNER

THIS view shows the Dining Hall filled and all ready to commence after grace is said. The number at present accommodated at meals is over 350.

The boarding department is under the charge of Mr. and Mrs. GEDDES. Three meals a day are served in the Hall. Breakfast at 8.5 A.M., preceded by morning prayers; dinner at 1.10 P.M.; and supper at 6.5 P.M., also preceded by evening prayers.

The commissariat arrangements for so large a number involves considerable expense and labour. Maize and milk and an allowance of meat twice a week form the staple food at the £8 or lowest table. The quantities of the chief articles of consumption yearly, including those sent to the Girls' School as well as those used by Europeans, are in round numbers as follows:—maize, 1200 bags; wheaten meal and flour, 300 bags; milk, 12,000 gallons; sheep, 800; oxen, 20; tea and coffee, 1400 lbs.; sugar, 11,000 lbs.; soap, 3000 lbs.

MUSTER FOR AFTERNOON WORK, JUNIORS

ONE of the standing objections on the part of some of the South African Colonists who are unfriendly to missions, is that the natives receive school education and no training in work. The rule that all shall work in some way, takes away all ground for such an objection. This would have been adopted though there had been no such objection. Over and above his regular class work each one must engage in some kind of regular work. There is of course a limit to such a rule, amongst those who come to receive education which is not gratuitous, but which is paid for by themselves.

Several views are given which show the large proportion which take part in out-door employment according to the season of the year.

72

MUSTER FOR AFTERNOON WORK

As described in another view, two hours' manual labour are required daily from all who are not indentured to any of the trades of carpentering, wagon-making, blacksmithing, printing, or bookbinding, or who have not some other duties assigned to them. As there is a large number to be employed, a muster in companies, each under a native captain, is necessary to prevent confusion and save time. This takes place at 2 P.M., or at 3 P.M. in the hottest weather. Each company then marches off to work. That varies according to the season in the fields and gardens, but there is always more than enough to do in improving and keeping in order the extensive grounds about the place.

THE BRICKFIELD

BRICKMAKING has not hitherto been taught as a regular trade at Lovedale, though a number of natives are so employed. Efforts are now, however, being made with a view to that end, in order to give the natives such knowledge as may enable them to improve their own dwellings; though the tenacity with which they adhere to the round hut is very great. The ease with which it is built, and the effects of old customs and associations have no doubt to do with this preference. It is a curious fact that the progressive races occupy rectangular dwellings; and when a native builds a square house it is generally an indication of a distinct advance.

For our present necessities and to prevent unwholesome overcrowding, two million bricks would not be more than sufficient.

IN THE FIELDS AND GARDENS

ALL those attending classes only have two hours daily of out-door work, on Saturdays three hours, or thirteen hours a week. The object is to induce habits of manual industry and prevent the African falling into the mistake very natural to him, that education consists in a knowledge of school-books. Health is another object. This work is, as already mentioned, sometimes in the fields connected with a large farm, at other times in the gardens, roads, and grounds round the buildings.

INTERIOR OF WAGON-MAKERS' SHOP

AFTER carpenter work, wagon-making is the favourite trade with natives. The ordinary Cape transport wagon is expected to carry from 8000 to 10,000 lbs. —between four and five tons—over rough roads, through stony rivers, and on journeys of almost any distance. It therefore requires strength, accurate measurements, and exact adjustment of wheels and some other parts, in order to secure satisfactory work. This always requires to be done under European supervision. The value of a good transport wagon varies from £70 to £100.

Latterly fewer wagons have been made at Lovedale, as steam and machinery have now been applied to their construction in colonial towns, and these appliances we have not yet been able to obtain. But that may yet be done, as soon as means for that object are got.

INTERIOR OF CARPENTERS' SHOP

AMONGST the handicrafts or industrial arts to which the Kaffir takes at first, none is more popular than that of carpenter work. There are generally more applicants than can be admitted, each in his own way anxious to learn that craft. Fairly good work can be generally produced, but the time taken is often excessive. It has been correctly said that the training of natives whose fathers and grand-fathers were barbarians is undoubtedly difficult work. Yet one master who has had long experience says: I am convinced there is mechanical ability in the natives of Africa, but at present it is dormant. Some say it is dead, but it is there if they would only use it. Mr. McGILLIVRAY has had charge of this department for twenty-two years.

INTERIOR OF PRINTING OFFICE

PRINTING was not at first a popular trade among the natives,—Kaffir experience not showing how a man could either be useful or earn a livelihood by arranging bits of lead in rows. It was only by a great effort that the first native printer was induced to learn that art. He afterwards learned telegraphy, and is now an ordained native preacher. But now there is less difficulty in obtaining apprentices, and later on these readily find employment in the Colony at twenty to thirty shillings a week. School and other books, both in Kaffir and English, are printed and bound at Lovedale, and the office has a good reputation for the quality of its printed work. Mr. FAIRLIE has been in charge of this department for over twenty years.

OLD WAGON-MAKERS' SHOP

VIEW showing the old wagon-makers' shop, and native apprentices at work on a Cape wagon and Scotch carts. A larger building is now used, and the above is converted into a dormitory.

The apprentices in all the different trades are taken on trial for three or six months. They must have some previous education. An intelligent workman cannot be made out of a man who can neither read nor write. Exceptional cases need not be regarded. If after trial they are found fairly satisfactory, they are indentured for four years. They receive a portion of their school education in the evening classes.

They are paid, along with board and lodging, at rates varying from eight shillings to twenty-one shillings a month. A small sum is kept as a drawback each year, which is repaid at the close of their apprenticeship, when they receive about £10—half in money and half in tools—if their trade admits of such an arrangement. With the carpenters and wagon-makers this can be carried out better than in some of the departments.

BLACK AND WHITE IN HARMONY

To keep the African always on the grindstone of work, or to be, as a non-missionary observer with more force than elegance remarked, always pounding Christianity into him, would be to defeat the object of the Mission, and render its success either limited or non-existent. Human nature is a curious thing. It will only stand so much of any process, occupation, or effort, within any given time. A change to something else is then necessary. Hence, though work rules the life of all who dwell at Lovedale, all rational relaxation and amusement are encouraged. And as all Africans are musical, there is a fairly good instrumental band. M. Germond, the son of a worthy French missionary in Basutoland, takes the musical responsibility as a relief from his other duties, and appears prominently in the centre of the group above. Black and white mingle in the band, as they do else-where and in the classes, though they sit at separate tables and have separate rooms. Many of the Europeans, from this contact, gain a lasting sympathy with the natives and acquire an interest in missions.

IN THE FIELDS

FOR the supply of food to over 500 native residents at Lovedale a large farm is cultivated. Maize and wheat are chiefly grown as grain. Millet, or as it is called in the country, Kaffir-corn, is grown and used chiefly by the natives; it is seldom grown by Europeans. Ploughing is seldom done by horses, but with teams of oxen, four, six, or eight. There were no horses in South Africa when the country was first discovered by the Portuguese; they were introduced by the Dutch East India Company. Among the Kaffirs the native name for a horse, *ihashe*, is simply a corruption of the English word. The natives are now extensive owners of horses, mostly of an inferior but hardy kind; and as a rule they are reckless and sometimes rather merciless riders.

MAIZE STORE

THE above shows a strong framework of timber, wire netting, and corrugated iron roof. This is used for drying and storing maize, of which, in good seasons, from 4000 to 5000 bags of maize cobs have to be so dealt with. After being gathered from the fields, it is exposed on the roof for ten days or more, and, when dry, is sent down through a shoot into the store, the sides of which are lined with strong wire netting to allow the air to pass freely through. Later on it is husked, or taken off the cob, by a machine driven by a steam-engine.

The entire produce of the Lovedale farm is used for the benefit of native boarders and the support of the Institution. The extent of land is nearly 2000 acres, of which 400 are arable and 300 are cultivated.

82

AFTERNOON SWEEPING UP

WHILE the older lads in different companies are employed in the fields, or on the roads, or at other occupations in the afternoons, a small company of juniors is detailed to the work of keeping the place clean and orderly, by a daily sweeping up. Some of that force are here represented. As already stated, the objects aimed at are, Godliness, Cleanliness, Industry, and Discipline. These are all practical things. They can neither be taught nor learned by mere theoretical instruction. Habits grow slowly, the best slowest of all. Hence the afternoon supplement of daily practical work in a great variety of forms.

WEDNESDAY AT NOON

HERE the class-rooms at twelve o'clock are emptying for a particular object. It is for what is known as the Wednesday noon-day prayer-meeting. At that hour all work in the place ceases. The blacksmith drops his hammer, the carpenter his saw, and the printer his types, the class-books are laid aside, and all assemble at a meeting which lasts less than an hour. In this Europeans and natives take part, and it is recognised as one of the pleasantest meetings in the place. Pecuniarily it involves a loss, as causing a deduction of fifty hours a week from the different trades departments, equal to the work of one man for a week.

There is an impression on the part of some good people that on account of a certain pervading atmosphere of work, or what they call secular employment, but which is in reality only a certain busy activity arising from the discouragement of idleness, there is less religious teaching than at most other mission stations. There can hardly be any station in South Africa at which, on week-days and Sundays, . there is more religious teaching and exposition of the Bible. The religious meetings of all kinds are very numerous. No one can attend them all. But the Wednesday meeting, which is one of them, is attended by all in the place, except those whose duties cannot for the time be interrupted.

AS THEY ARE AT HOME IN THEIR OWN VILLAGES

A GROUP, chiefly of native women and girls in the uncivilised state, taken in one of their own villages a short distance from Lovedale. The dresses, armlets, and anklets belong to what is called the Red Kaffir condition. Its adherents hold to the old customs, have not yet accepted Christianity, and are conservative in most of their ways, preferring the old state to the new. They are, however, reached by the missionary when he itinerates, and they gradually begin to attend the regular services in the native churches.

AS THEY BECOME UNDER CHRISTIANITY AND CIVILISATION

THE above shows the front of the buildings of the Girls' School, with a number of the pupils, girls and young women, in groups on the grass. The dark figures in the foreground are also native women who have come to sell something in baskets, which they carry, native fashion, on their heads. The difference which education and Christianity produce on a native girl, in expression, dress, and bearing, is very marked. When this view was taken, the school was under charge of the late Mrs. MUIRHEAD, who, with some of the lady teachers, are seen at the right.

THE GIRLS' SCHOOL

ANOTHER view of a portion of the Girls' School as it was less than a year ago. Amongst the lady teachers who appear is Miss DODDS, who has charge, and Miss BARNLEY, who has been as missionary at Lovedale for more than a dozen years.

To the homes whence they come, all these girls return after a few years. That they should carry no good influences with them as the result of Christian teaching, nor any of the domestic habits to which they have been trained, in order to improve their own dwellings, and make their native homes more comfortable and orderly, is surely very improbable. The contrary is known to be the case with most. And thus slowly the leaven of Christianity spreads; and where it comes, many other beneficent influences in the family life follow in its train.

NATIVE WEDDING PARTY

THIS is a very accurate representation of an ordinary native marriage party, in which the chief actors have become Christians, and some of their kinsfolk and acquaintances have not. The two conditions of native social life and of moral and material progress are here brought into sharp contrast. Some would perhaps prefer the sombre picturesqueness of the outside group. All that need be said is, that Picturesque Heathenism is best at a distance, and most agreeable in a picture. That Christianity is favourable to all the moral virtues, and that soap is a product of civilisation, really ends the argument, as all actually acquainted with the two states in the concrete reality very well know.

Natives spend a great deal of money on their marriages, sometimes when they cannot well afford the expenditure. Missionary conferences have entreated, advised, and denounced this expenditure, but, if the bride or her friends can manage it, she will appear in white satin, white kid gloves, and all other adornments to match. There is also prolonged feasting—an ox, two or three sheep or goats, a bag of sugar, and coffee *ad libitum* being considered necessary.

88

GROUP OF UNCIVILISED NATIVES

THE above shows a group of natives, chiefly women, as yet untouched by education or Christianity. It requires to be looked at in contrast with the next two or three groups. Whatever may be said about the results of missions, there can be no question on this point—that the effect of missionary teaching in every land always ameliorates the lot of woman. No religion does this so directly, quickly, and really as the religion of Jesus Christ. Most false religions rather lend their sanction to her degradation and oppression.

NATIVE GIRLS, SUPPORTED BY HOME FRIENDS

SOME friends of missions, and also some Sunday schools, prefer to give their contributions to the support of individual natives in whose welfare they take an interest. There are always some such at Lovedale. Eight pounds a year provides for their board and education. The above shows a group of native girls who have been aided in this way. Many who have been thus taught become themselves, later on, female teachers in mission schools. But we cannot promise that such will be the case with all, as some have not the ability, and others have not the inclination to teach.

GALLA GIRLS—RESCUED SLAVES

THE above shows a group of Galla girls rescued from an Arab slave-dhow, as described in a previous picture. The histories of these girls, most of whom were mere children when first captured, have a sad similarity. Some do not remember the names of their parents, though others give connected accounts of their early years and the circumstances of their being first taken and sold. Sometimes it was a raid on the village, in which many of the men were killed and the women and children carried off as slaves. Others were kidnapped and carried off. One is said to have been sold for a horse, another for a debt, another for a sword, and another for a certain number of pieces of salt.

CLASS ROOMS, GIRLS' SCHOOL

THIS low building of the bungalow type forms one of the class-rooms, and also affords two rooms for industrial work, in which sewing of all kinds is taught, and laundry work. Of this group, about half belongs to the Industrial Department. The value of the work done last year—for washing, dressing, and sewing, was close on £300. Mrs. BENNIE has had charge of this industrial work, and efficiently conducted it for some years past.

PART OF GIRLS' SCHOOL

THIS view shows part of the front of the Girls' School and a few gathering for the muster for out-door work in the afternoon. Such out-door work is not carried out to the same extent as in the boys' institution, as all the indoor work of the place is done by the girls themselves, no servants being kept. The training of the girls is thus domestic and industrial, as well as purely educational. It is necessary to teach them to read and write, but it is as need-ful to teach them to sew and wash, to make bread, to cook and scrub, and become fitter to be the wives of native missionaries, teachers, and farmers. To educate the young men only would be doing half the necessary work.

LOVEDALE BUILDINGS IN THE DISTANCE

THIS view across a maize field shows about half the buildings of Lovedale. Those to the right form the older portion, while to the left appear those more recently erected. None of the dwelling-houses or workshops are shown here, and to the above must be added a number of buildings both to the east and west of those shown in the picture. The earliest temporary erections were wattle and daub, just as in Central Africa, wood wattles and grass are at first set up. These give place to houses of very rough stone or sun-dried or burnt brick. Later on, better buildings of dressed stone appear. These indicate the permanent occupation of the country for missionary purposes. Wattle and daub in the end is the most expensive, owing to the necessity for constant repairs.

The never-ceasing, though gradual growth of the place, has involved us in continuous building. Had the later necessities of the place been better known in those earlier days, more regularity of plan could have been followed both in buildings and in their general arrangement.

NEAR THE GIRLS' SCHOOL

THE above shows some of the grounds near the Girls' School, and native girls carrying clothes to the laundry below the water-course. The contrast between a group of girls so employed and attired, and a group of native women in the red blanket and clay of the purely heathen state is very great. That however is only the external difference, which is still more marked, as has elsewhere been stated, in the expression and general bearing, which becomes in every way more pleasant and more womanly. Such training in household and domestic work, seems just what is necessary to bring out many of those feminine traits of character which are more or less undeveloped in the uncivilised condition.

There is another effect. We find that these women who have received education themselves, become as mothers of families always anxious for the education of their children, and often make great sacrifices to secure that end. Many of them have already raised the standard of living in their own homes, and sent their children to the Institute where they were themselves trained.

95

AVENUES FROM GIRLS' SCHOOL

THESE two avenues connect the Girls' School with the rest of Lovedale lying a little to the east. Natives learn by what they see as well as by what they hear, and the remarks quoted in a previous page about external influences in education are also applicable here. There is only one way of teaching the native people to improve their dwellings and make their own villages pleasanter places, and that is, by showing what may be done by a little daily care, cleanliness, and industry. Hence our care about the surroundings of the station as well as other minor arrangements. Though many thousands have renounced heathenism, and a very much larger number have become civilised, it would be wrong to say that the majority of the native population have accepted Christianity. The great bulk of the natives are still without any religion, and hold firmly to the old customs and superstitions of their forefathers; though there is a steady advance year by year. The little leaven makes its way silently and slowly, but all the more surely. And among the influences promoting or opposing this advance, none is more potent and silent than the influence of the women. From this arises the importance of giving them a Christian education. It was begun late, long after many efforts had been made for the education of the opposite sex. But now most missionary societies are attending carefully to this section of their work.

AVENUE AT LOVEDALE

THIS was formerly one of the approaches to Lovedale. It was that generally taken by visitors, who came from many quarters to see the place. Missionaries and others come to see for themselves. During each year we see many people, and as far as we can, for the sake of the work as well as for themselves, we endeavour to welcome all who come. We have had strangers from Barbadoes and China in the same week. The Governors of the Colony, when on the frontier, generally make Lovedale a stage on the journey. Most of them have visited it. SIR BARTLE FRERE came during the last Kaffir war, 1877-78, and more recently, SIR HENRY and LADY LOCH. One of the most distinguished visitors was the hero of Khartoum, General GORDON. His message to the native lads is still remembered and preserved in writing.

AVENUE FROM MAIN ROAD

SOME years ago the ground here was a bare field. As the place grew, new roads were necessary, and where these are made trees are generally planted, and other improvements made. It was probably this which led Inspector-General Ross to speak of the external influence of Lovedale on the native mind as an 'education. The well-kept walks, the rows of trees growing up on all sides, the well-filled water-furrows, the farm, the native chapel, and a series of minor civilising influences, are likely sooner or later to tell on the native character; to give them a higher ideal of life than their own; to make them know and understand the value of work; to use their senses, their hands, their general faculties, their bone and muscle, in a profitable fashion; to develop in them a taste for knowledge, which is to them a very wonderful thing; and to make the pursuit of it a profit instead of a disagreeable, repelling toil.'

LOVEDALE HOUSES—DOMIRA

THIS house, formerly called Block Drift, was the old British Residency in the early days of the military occupation of Kaffraria, and when Captain STRETCH, whose name has been previously mentioned, was Diplomatic Agent with the Gaikas. In its immediate neighbourhood occurred the meeting between Sandilli, the paramount chief of the Kaffirs, and the Governor of the colony, in the war of 1846-47. There was a good deal of fighting in the immediate neighbourhood; and a mile distant are the ruins of a large encampment known as Fort Hare. It is now the property of Lovedale.

Block Drift and its adjoining lands were purchased for a thousand pounds and given to Lovedale by JOHN STEPHEN, Esq., of Glasgow.

LOVEDALE HOUSES

THE above shows a portion of two houses situated in one of the long avenues found about the place. Most of the trees in this avenue are English oaks, and they have all been planted within comparatively recent years. These and many other English trees, all except those which require a cold winter, thrive well. The English oak has found a new home in South Africa, and specially in the western province of the colony, where, it is said, it grows nearly twice as fast with a foliage twice as dense as at home, and an acorn nearly double the usual home size. And there is nothing to show that the wood, under skilful treatment, would not be as good as the oak of Europe.

Some of the trees close by are Australian blue gums. In a congenial soil, and with a plentiful supply of water, some species of these trees will grow from six to eight feet in a year. The blue gum is frequently planted at mission stations in treeless districts, and the group of tall trees generally indicates to the traveller the position of the Mission at a distance long before the buildings can be made out.

A GROUP AT THEIR OWN HOME

THE hut shown above is the normal dwelling of the native people of South Africa. In this case it is more like the hut built by the Fingoes, with higher walls of wattle and daub, and a higher door than the old Kaffir hut which had low walls of grass, and the thatch of the roof continued down to the ground. The door was correspondingly low, and it was necessary to creep in order to enter the dwelling.

The group outside—unpromising and uncivilised as they may appear—are each and all probably better than they look. The Kaffirs, as a race, will stand comparison with the men of most other uncivilised races. In the old fighting days, they were described by war correspondents as magnificent savages. And a non-missionary writer of the present day describes them quite accurately and justly, as 'generally fine, powerful, able-bodied men, reserved and self-possessed in manner, but courteous and polite and sensible of kindness and consideration.' All which, as traits of the Kaffirs, the writer of this page, after nearly thirty years' contact with them, can verify, as being according to truth and reality.

KAFFIR CUSTOMS—THE ABAKWETA

THERE are many curious customs among the Kaffirs, as among all primitive races. An account of these would require a small volume. As is well known, it is often difficult to secure photographs of native customs; and some even of the native chiefs at first refuse to allow any photograph to be taken of themselves from a superstitious dread of the results—though after they have got over their alarm they are generally well pleased with what is to them a very wonderful process. These views are probably the first of the kind which have been published in this country, and the photographer regarded it as a piece of good fortune that he had secured them. Though there is considerable similarity, three views are given, partly to obtain space for a very brief description of one or the most peculiar and picturesque of Kaffir customs—and one which is most deeply seated in their national life. It has been called partly a religious and partly a civil rite—though there is very little religion in it. Most of their superstitions and many of their customs are opposed to the Gospel, and to the morality it teaches.

Continued on next page.

KAFFIR CUSTOMS—THE ABAKWETA

The above represents the *ukutshila* or dance which accompanies the rite of circumcision as that is practised amongst some of the South African tribes. By this rite and the ceremonies which accompany it, lads of a certain age are admitted to the standing of men, and are added to the fighting force of the tribe.

Those thus initiated are called *Abakweta*. Several kraals or villages unite to celebrate this custom. For some weeks these lads live by themselves. They are supplied with food by their friends and are looked after by one man, who takes charge of them during that period. They are covered from head to foot with white clay, which makes them look as if they were whitewashed. This gives them a very ghastly appearance, and they are commonly called the white boys by Europeans. They also wear the strange head-dresses which appear in the picture, and a sort of kilt or half tunic, made of the fronds of a dwarf or wild date-palm. The weight of the latter is often very great. It adds to the severity of the muscular exercise which these dancers undergo, and the

Continued on next page.

U

KAFFIR CUSTOMS—THE ABAKWETA

perspiration runs down their bodies in dark streams through the white clay. The object is to develop their strength and endurance. These *Abakweta* go round different villages, and there is a good deal of singing, dancing, feasting, and beating of drums of dried hide.

After several weeks, the white clay is washed off in the nearest river, red clay takes its place, and a new kaross or blanket is given to each. All the old clothing, such as it is, is also burned. The lads are then assembled to receive advice and instruction from the old men as to their new duties. They are now to act as men, being acknowledged as such. They are to obey their Chief and defend the tribe against its enemies; to provide for their parents and other relatives; to maintain the customs of their forefathers and other ways of the tribe; and to be hospitable to their friends and to those who may have a claim upon them. They also receive presents of assegais, and cattle according to the wealth of their relatives, as well as other things to enable them to make a

Continued on next page.

GROUP OF SPECTATORS AT THE ABAKWETA

beginning in life. Cattle are then slaughtered and the ceremony concludes with a great feast.

The young Kaffir looks forward to this period as the time when he will be no longer a boy sent to look after the calves, but will be recognised as a man of the tribe. No taunt that one Kaffir can address to another, cuts so deep as to hint that he has never passed through this rite and that he is therefore still a boy merely and not a man. This custom stands in the way of missionary work, not because it is in any way evil in itself, but because of its associations. There are various other practices connected with this rite which cannot be described here. In the pictures the *Abakweta* look, as some one remarked, like little fairies or ballet dancers, but they are not innocent little fairies for all that.

The above view represents a group of spectators who are watching the dancers and waiting for the feast.

WATERFALL ON THE RIVER OHUMIE

THE new effort at the present time is the reorganisation of the Industrial Departments, so as to give a much better kind of teaching in the different trades. The necessity for this as a part of industrial or technical education is now recognised at home. It is intended to utilise this waterfall as a means for introducing power to drive machinery in the workshops, for the supply of water, and for other purposes. The waterfall is nearly a mile distant, but it is believed that by a turbine and dynamo with an overhead wire, it may be practicable to carry the power so produced into the Lovedale workshops. This would involve an expenditure of two thousand pounds, but it would make a great and beneficial change. It would modernise the old methods of working wholly by hand labour —with its result of limited production, and greatly increased cost of the articles produced. Some friends of the Mission may possibly be induced to aid us in this effort; a beginning has already been made.

EPILOGUE

FTER so much has been said in a missionary book about education and secular occupation and manual employment, a final word about our primary aim, though that has already been stated, may not be out of place. And for that we may adapt the language of a recent writer on Lovedale, as expressing our missionary creed and practice, and say :—

We declare plainly that the Institute exists to teach the natives the religion of Jesus Christ. We care for books and tools, workshops and class-rooms and field-work only as means to open up the mind to the more ready acceptance of the great truths of the Bible, and afford room for the practical exhibition of these truths in daily life. We believe in conversion, and regard it as the highest result of our labours. We believe in loyalty to Christ as the highest ideal and the most inspiring belief. We often fall below our ideal, but we begin again. We try to fit young native men and women to become useful and progressive citizens, and to become missionaries of civilisation and Christianity to all the natives of Africa. Every teacher in his own depart-ment is expected to be occupied directly or indirectly with this aim. Some of our work is depressing and occasionally disappointing. It involves some strain and exertion because the staff is too small, and the influences of climate, though it is excellent, have their effect. The thermometer seldom falls below 50 degrees Fahr., and often runs up rapidly to 105 degrees.

But we have a great deal of encouragement from Christian friends at home, and also in the results of Christian teaching as these appear

among the people themselves.   If also there are some in the colony who
are unfriendly to missions—and unreasonably so from prejudice or want
of information,—there is a large section of Christian people who are
in entire sympathy with missionary work.   And here it would be ungrateful
not to acknowledge the indebtedness of all true missionary work to the press
of the Colony.   Critical it sometimes is and justly so, in applying to all
missionary work the canons of practical common sense.   But the fact remains
beyond any doubt that the best and ablest portions of the Colonial press are
entirely on the side of missions ; and wholly in sympathy with any reasonable method in missionary effort, having for its object the elevation of the
people.

All this being so, what remains but to gratefully acknowledge all help
that is given ; to thank God for the opportunity of work ; to take courage,
and endeavour to make whatever failures have marred the past the means to
better results for the future—trusting in God's promise and purpose about
this world, which is His world and not ours,—He being the Chief Worker
in it.

FINIS

Printed by T. and A. CONSTABLE, Printers to Her Majesty
at the Edinburgh University Press

Lightning Source UK Ltd.
Milton Keynes UK
UKHW020734140922
408851UK00005B/558